19/06

£6=

# Rail Tales of the Unexpected

# Rail Tales of the Unexpected

K Westcott Jones

BCA

LONDON · NEW YORK · SYDNEY · TORONTO

First published by
David St John Thomas Publisher
PO Box 4, Nairn, Scotland IV12 4HU

This edition published 1992
by BCA by arrangement with
David St John Thomas Publisher

CN 3382

Typeset by XL Publishing Services, Nairn
Printed in Great Britain by Billing & Son, Worcester
for David St John Thomas Publishers
PO Box 4, Nairn, Scotland IV12 4HU

# Contents

5

# Introduction

ALTHOUGH railways are the most orderly and best supervised form of transport the world has ever known, they add to their eternal fascination by very occasional aberrations. At their most serious, these lapses result in horrendous disasters, well chronicled in official reports and classic accident books.

But unexpected occurrences, not leading to disaster, often go unrecorded and it is the main objective of this book to tell the sometimes amusing, sometimes tragic, consequences of them. In some cases aspects of well known disasters have been highlighted. In one instance a strange flash of intuition which came over a passenger arriving at Ladybank on the Dundee train one windy night in 1879, and the better known instance of the man whose carriage came to collect him just as the train was leaving Leuchars Junction.

Some small acts by passengers have passed into legendary history, such as the man travelling to London Bridge during the black-out of World War II who opened the compartment door in the belief that the train had already reached the terminus. Other passengers shouted at him in alarm but he stepped out and fell onto the tracks, luckily avoiding the live rails. He is said to have clambered back in, somewhat bruised, apologising for his stupidity, and then opened the other door to fall out again on what he hoped was the platform side!

There is the story on the Elham Valley line in Kent, or at least there was when that charming branch line from Folkestone to Canterbury was still functioning, of a giant rail-mounted gun used for firing back at German positions across the Channel. The first time it was used in anger, after a particularly savage bombardment against Dover, the soldiers around it - their ears and eyes protected from flash and noise - hefted their massive shell, heard it fired by the men on the flat wagon, and turned a few seconds later to behold empty tracks! The enormous recoil had driven the vehicle and its gun backwards at speed into the mouth of a tunnel.

I doubt if there is a mile of railway track in Britain and Ireland, even including sidings, where something unusual has not happened. Every tunnel, too, has its stories, the light at the end of them all too often being a train coming the other way. Charles Dickens wrote about ghosts on the railway and was an early fan of trains until the Staplehurst disaster involved him, very unexpectedly.

There is a tendency to believe that faults, delays, points failures, derailments, signalling failures, missed station stops, fires and late arrivals are all part of the modern railway scene, not encountered in the great days of the British system up to 1940. This is by no means the case, as a study of pre-war newspaper clippings will show. More light is shed by the media these days on errors and disasters than used to be the practice by newspapers and BBC Radio. But they were recorded, even lateness.

When a bad accident happened in the 1930s, newspaper editorials often began by expressing sympathy to the Railway Company concerned (the Castle Cary disaster on the LNER in 1937, or the Southern Railway derailment at Sevenoaks in 1927, for example). The attitude to railways was very different. They were then the pride and joy of every Briton and to a large extent the envy of the whole world. We must not forget that they were generally profitable, Great Western Debentures being regarded as better than Gilt-edged stocks. Only the LNER was in financial trouble, but it still paid slim dividends on its First Preference. In its later years, the Southern Railway Company (the most successful transport company in Europe, with a free scrip issue in 1935), yielded no less than eight percent on its Deferred Stock.

However, with manned signal boxes, pre-war errors were usually human and fortunately rare. Train cancellations were very exceptional, usually pre-arranged due to fog service working. If steam engines broke down - and they did quite often even in the great days - they could usually limp to a station where help was at hand. Derailments of four-wheeler, chain-coupled goods wagons were frequent, but armies of rail workers could and did clear the lines very quickly. Station masters kept lists of men who could be called out to help at all hours, shovelling snow or righting wagons, for half a crown, and before there is an outcry of 'slave labour' let it be said that this sum bought an otherwise unemployed man a three pound joint of Argentine beef and a pint of beer.

Cutbacks today have meant fewer workers available, and a naive belief in the wonderful workings of electronics. Signal and points failures these days are the prime curse of the system, from the West Highlands (with the radio staff in the cab sometimes afflicted by mountain shadow) to the cable faults so often occurring on the busy Network Southeast lines. The officially unexpected happens so frequently in this field it is becoming expected.

No doubt the first unexpected occurrence on a railway was the fatal accident to Huskisson at Liverpool and Manchester trials in 1829. But even more unexpected and disturbing was the statement by a local priest at the opening of the world's first railway tunnel on the Canterbury and Witsable Railway in 1830.

The priest demanded that a gate be fixed to the tunnel mouths so that 'no hanky panky', as he put it, could take place. For the seven years that he held office the rule was enforced, causing all trains to stop, open and close the gate, traverse the tunnel, and repeat the procedure. Tyler's Hill Tunnel is still there, on the disused line, but little attention is paid to the site considering it was the first railway tunnel in all the world. The locomotive *Invicta* is preserved, however, and on show in the Canterbury Museum.

Those English cities with medieval walls and gates had become liberal when the railways arrived on the scene, so the opening and shutting of gates at curfew was already a thing of the past. Not so in Basle, however, where the city gates continued to be shut at dark until 1850 and the evening train from Paris had to halt and whistle for them to be opened to allow it through into the station within the city walls.

Charles Dickens features on the railway scene both from his stories and his descriptions, but the Staplehurst disaster was for him the end of the line. As is well known the permanent way gang had removed an 8ft length of track on which Dickens's express was travelling (with his lady friend) from Folkstone, having crossed by paddle steamer from Boulogne. It became seriously derailed with considerable loss of life.

The word 'unexpected' turned up in evidence given by the foreman of the permanent way gang. 'We knew about the Tidal train (the term in use in those days for Boat Train - now Channel Train) coming up from Dover at 4 o'clock but the sudden arrival of the Tidal train from Folkstone at 2 o'clock was *unexpected*.'

Breakfasting aboard the *Golden Hind* from Plymouth on a stormy day as it traversed the tunnels and seashore near Dawlish led to an unexpected trickle of sea water from the window into a bowl of porridge! On that same line, where the 'hi-tech' of the 1840s led to the unexpected action by rats eating the tallow of the atmospheric system, 'hi-tech' of the 1980s - deluged with sea water - had a colour light signal flashing red and green every few seconds.

However, the optimists think that the 'Iron Horse has entered Space Age technology' and these expectations could transform the nineteenth century Iron Horse into a twenty-first century 'Silicon Stallion'. But the experts must watch out as best possible for the unexpected.

---

## Acknowledgments

---

NUMEROUS sources have been tapped to research the contents of this book, and I am indebted in particular to Mr Desmond Martin, who spent much of the 1950s and early 1960s travelling the length and breadth of Britain by rail - when he was not helping on the Talyllyn Railway. He was an active member of the Stephenson Locomotive Society and shared that organisation's experiences on special trains during the latter days of scheduled steam working.

My thanks are also due to Mr Tony Hudson, a noted photographer who has often accompanied me on railway journeys at home and abroad, and to Mr John Hawkes, a railway officer of pre-war days whose experiences were manifold.

Various public relations officers have also given time and effort digging into early files. On InterCity, Messrs. Peter Northfield, david Potter, and Mike Bowler have dredged their memories and checked some facts. On regional railways, Mr Peter Hipkin is especially thanked for his descriptions of 'Saturday Night Manouevres' in his native East Anglia. Mr Peter Semmens, formerly deputy keeper at York Railway Museum, has also offered valuable assistance and advice.

# 1

# The King and the B12

A June day in north east Essex may well be bright and sunny but 14 June 1951 was sultry and very warm, with very little breeze. Men working in shirt sleeves were stringing flags and bunting along the canopies of the platforms at Parkeston Quay, and they were feeling the heat. The light zephyrs scarcely stirred the bunting and paper crowns hardly moved.

A King was coming. There was much activity at the Eastern Region packet port on the Stour which in those days, only three years after nationalisation, was still regarded as a London and North Eastern Railway 'Company' base. It was full of pride and efficiency, with a large but mainly contented railway staff handling the trains and ships.

The King who was on his way would be on the bridge of a ship flying the flag of his country, Denmark. King Frederick served at sea aboard ships of the East Asiatic Company, and obtained the necessary certificates to qualify as a navigating officer. Whenever he crossed the North Sea from Esbjerg in vessels of the DFDS Company, one of which was named after him, he lost no opportunity in doing a stint on the bridge.

But King Frederick had another great interest. He was a keen railway enthusiast with a particular affection for steam locomotives. Indeed, when he died his will was specific about his funeral train - it was to be hauled by two of his favourite engines, the Swedish-built Pacifics. In the event there was only one in good operative condition in Denmark at the time. The authorities had to send urgently to Sweden for another one to be transported by train ferry to take its place at the head of the long heavy train, filled with sad mourners which conveyed his body from Copenhagen to Roskilde, traditional burial place for Danish crowned heads.

King Frederick was, however, a fit and active man back in 1951. He frequently crossed to England on both official and semi-official visits. This was a semi-official occasion, without much ceremony apart from handshakes and welcomes from the Lord Leiutenant of Essex and the railway managers at Parkeston Quay. One royal coach was attached to the regular *Scandinavian*, the boat train meeting the DFDS ship, and it was in this unit from the Royal Train that he was due to travel, accompanied by his small retinue.

Gathered in the noon-day heat beside the royal coach, the King suddenly detached himself and, accompanied by an aide with a camera, set off briskly along the platform. Watchers outside the station buildings made slight bows as his tall figure strode past while those of us who knew he was going along to the locomotive followed him at a discreet distance. There were no security scares or over-cautious bodyguarding in those days, and in any case the King of Denmark was among friends.

There at the head of the train, gleaming in the sunshine and in pristine condition, stood B12 4-6-0 No 61567. King Frederick took the camera from his aide, and spectators stood well back so that he would be able to get uncluttered pictures.

Most of us there on that June day knew that the King had sent a request for a 1500 to haul his train to London. He was well aware that their numbers were getting short, although they were being used on fast trains from

Liverpool Street to Southend and on secondary trains along the East Suffolk line. No 61567 had been specially prepared on five days notice. We had seen the engine arrive from a final sprucing at Dovercourt Shed and back on to the *Scandinavian*, normally in those days a turn for one of the ubiquitous Thompson B1s or a *Sandringham*.

When the King returned to his special accommodation it was by no means clear if all the official reception party had known what he was going to do. The Lord Lieutenant's face wore a very puzzled expression, although the Port Manager looked pleased and satisfied.

When whistles blew and hundreds of heads disappeared from the various carriage windows, the King and his retinue boarded the royal coach loaned by his friend King George V1. The inside cylinders of the handsome veteran up front, (once, some thirty years earlier, a regular on the eighty minute Hook of Holland boat trains) began to turn. As a passenger aboard, I recorded progress, and it was a good run along the estuary of the Stour to join the main line at Manningtree.

Unlike King Boris of Bulgaria, almost a fanatical railway enthusiast who had done quite terrible things on the footplate of engines hauling the *Orient Express* across his country, and had made imperious demands of the LMS in 1937 on a run to Crewe, King Frederick had not exerted pressure to ride with the driver and fireman but it is reported that he, too, kept a careful note of the journey to London. It has to be assumed that special clearances were afforded the *Scandinavian* that day, but the B12, with twelve coaches, one very heavy giving an all-up weight of about 420 tons, reached Liverpool Street in seventy-eight minutes, twice touching eighty miles an hour. The King was delighted and said so during a three minute talk to the driver.

# 2

# Second Time at Winsford

ON Boxing Day, 1962, three men were travelling south from a short holiday in Scotland in a crowded train from Glasgow. In those days British Railways operated trains on 26 December, obtaining full loads. Only in more recent years has the system been closed down for the two full days of the Christmas holiday period, a decision which must have played its part in extending the amount of time taken off work by Britons (in contrast to their European competitors).

They were all railway enthusiasts and had been in Scotland to indulge their hobby. The talk in their compartment ranged across many aspects of rail operation, and as the *Mid-Day Scot*, forging along through misty murk in freezing conditions between Warrington and Crewe, one of them re-told the story of the Winsford disaster.

The train, in fact, came to a halt near the scene of that devastating crash of April 1948. There was time for the historian to recount to his companions the events of a few minutes after midnight on 17 April 1948, before the *Mid-Day Scot* hauled by an English Electric diesel began to move forward again.

The Winsford accident was the first major accident on the newly nationalised British Railways, occurring just three and a half months into the public ownership regime. The 5.40pm express from Glasgow had been brought to a stand by a young soldier who had pulled the communication cord at Winsford Junction. The fireman from *Princess Arthur of Connaught* climbed down and walked back along the train while the guard sought the compartment of the pulled cord. It was, of course, very dark and their lamps were dim (in fact the guard's light went out and had to be re-lit). The two men took rather a long time and detonators were not laid to protect the train for some fifteen minutes.

Just two minutes later the up Glasgow Postal, running late and doing about seventy miles an hour under clear signals, came into sight. The driver of Pacific No 6251 *City of Nottingham* heard a detonator explode under his wheels and then saw a faint red light being waved. He immediately shut off steam and jammed on his brakes, reducing speed by about 25 mph before the inevitable impact which shattered the two rear coaches of the Glasgow passenger train, killing twenty four people.

There had been signalling errors as well as delays in protecting the train stopped in the dark between sections. But a feature of the crash was that passengers in the front coaches of the 5.40pm did not realise that the bump they felt was a major accident.

As he finished his story of the Winsford disaster of some fourteen and a half years previously, the *Mid-Day Scot* began to move towards Crewe. The three men peered out of the windows into the darkness where firm snow showed up between the tracks as the train cantered gently along, reaching about 25mph. Then the brakes went on sharply.

The men, who were lucky to have been riding in almost the last of thirteen well-filled coaches, felt a considerable bump.'Looks like we hit something,' exclaimed one of them.

They had. Their train had run into the back of the 4.45pm from Liverpool to Birmingham, which had been halted at signals ahead of them. Their diesel had smashed the last two coaches, just as in 1948 and eighteen people died.

A drunk lying in the corridor did not stir, but the friends in the compartment, sliding back the top of the window, knew something serious was amiss. They could hear their diesel idling and from the rear of the train they detected shouts and saw people down on the track with lanterns. Ahead in the murk there was chaos.

Many minutes passed with no positive news but then a Red Cross man came down their corridor, carrying an urn of tea. He tried to awaken the drunk without success before pulling back the door of their compartment. 'Tea, gentlemen,' he said, setting up paper cups. A visitor came in from the next compartment. 'Please make mine coffee,' the newcomer requested. 'There are dead and dying up front,' the Red Cross man bellowed. 'You're lucky to get anything - take a cup of tea or nothing.'

The next arrival was a travelling ticket collector, who asked to see the tickets. In response to many questions he replied that there was a bit of a mishap, but they must stay in the train.

Two hours later, the train began to move backwards down the line, hauled by a diesel engine which had come out of the frosty darkness. Two railway staff came through the corridors, calling out, 'British Railways regret that there may be some delay.'

There was indeed some delay, while the train made its slow way back to Hartford where buses awaited the attenuated *Mid-Day Scot*. Passengers were taken to Crewe for a train to Euston, where the survivors counted themselves fortunate to be only three and a half hours late. Lightning had indeed struck twice, to cause *Winsford II*, in this case the fault of a Scottish driver who had deliberately passed a red light after failing to get through on a lineside telephone.

A curious fact emerged during coverage by the media

of this disaster and the 1948 one at Winsford. Although the young soldier who had pulled the communication cord was not to blame for the crash (a stalled train should have been protected) he was attacked for his selfishness. It upset him so much that when he left the army he decided to devote his life to railway safety. He became a signalman and has only recently retired after a long, accident-free career.

# 3

# Ninety Days from Inverness to Portree

ON a wet September afternoon in the year 1880, a gallant little 2-4-0 tender engine built by David Jones, the Highland Railway chief engineer who served twenty-six years in the post, simmered at an Inverness platform. She was due to haul a rake of six-wheel coaches over the Dingwall and Skye Railway to Strome Ferry, in those days the end of the line some seventy-two miles from Inverness.

Recently taken over by the Highland Railway, which had always worked it, the Skye and Dingwall provided a steamer service from Strome Ferry to Portree, Skye's small capital, and to Stornoway in distant Lewis. It was to be another seventeen years before the Highland scraped up enough money to build the difficult extension to Kyle of Lochalsh, only half a mile across the water from the looming mass of Skye.

Meanwhile, small steamers ploughed their way down the fjord-like waters of Loch Carron, out across the wider waters of the Inner Sound, around Scalpay Island and through the Narrows of Raasey to Portree, a trip of about forty-three miles. The longer, rougher journey across the Minch to Stornoway, served three times a week, took all night.

Until the Highland Railway took over and acquired more ships, the service to Stornoway had been only once a week, supplemented by a smaller connecting steamer from Portree owned by the local Hutcheson Company. Now there were three, the *Carham*, *Ferret* and *Whippet*, one more than was strictly required to operate the sea routes. *Ferret*, built in 1872 by Thompsons of Glasgow, was an iron-screw vessel of some 347 tons, well appointed by the standards of the day, with cross-trees on her raked masts which enabled her to be sail-assisted for longer voyages. She even had some primitive berth accommodation, and occasionally undertook profitable charters well away from Highland waters. She had been to the Humber, and just before coming back to Strome Ferry to take the service for which the Highland train was waiting on that September afternoon had been down to Cardiff.

It is not known how many passengers joined the train at Inverness, for many would have made relatively local journeys, alighting at Dingwall - County Town of Ross and Cromarty - or in ones and twos at remote spots along the lonely scenic railway to the west. But we do know that seventeen persons, four of them named McLeod, were bound for Portree that day.

Many residents of Skye were and still are named McLeod for Dunvegan Castle, on the north western side of the Big Island, was the seat of the clan McLeod. The elderly Dame Flora McLeod of McLeod actually lived there as a small child in 1880. Four of her father's clanspeople were on their way to the island, having been shopping or doing other business in Inverness.

The little 2-4-0 reached Dingwall in under half an hour, then after watering hauled her train away into the great hills, doing the difficult job she was built for, and breasting Raven's Rock Summit in fine style despite the slippery rails and increasing wind. Halted at Achnasheen on the passing loop and taking more water, the train was crossed by the up service from Strome Ferry. From information given by the crew and, no doubt, some of the passengers, they knew the steamer *Ferret* was at her berth and duly waiting for the Inverness train. Weather conditions were described as poor but tolerable.

It was downhill almost all the way, after the Achnasheen stop to Strome Ferry. It took less than an hour, and there they saw the neat little Highland steamer at her quay the other side of the station building. A strong wind was whipping the smoke from her elegant raked funnel and raising white horses on the surface of Loch Carron, but the weather was nothing exceptional, certainly not bad by the standards often experienced in deep winter in this region.

Helped by porters, who were a ubiquitous breed on the railways of Victorian times, the seventeen passengers for Portree crossed the platform and up the gangplank of the *Ferret*. She was not scheduled to go on to Stornoway on this particular day. However, other passengers alighted from the train to take a small ferry across the loch to villages and crofts inland from the other shore. In those days the population of Wester Ross was twice what it is today, while Skye had three times as many people.

The empty train at Strome Ferry remained at the platform, her engine serviced, coaled and watered, at the local shed of the then tiny terminus, before returning to Inverness as the first run of the day, picking up ferry passengers and those coming in from Stornoway and Portree aboard one of the two other Highland steamers.

*Ferret* steamed away into the growing darkness of the wet and windy September evening. Her passengers went below into the wooden saloon with its trestle tables to eat an evening meal, the earlier the better in case the waters on Inner Sound should prove particularly unfriendly. Watchers saw that the ship had a deckload of coal, no doubt bought very cheaply in Cardiff, plus some timber.

People on the lochside at Strome Ferry and further down at the tiny village of Plockton saw the handsome little steamer out-lined against the high hills of the Applecross Peninsula before she disappeared into the wet twilight. They were never to see her again. Indeed *Ferret* was making her last voyage in Scotland.

In the nineteenth century before the advent of electric signal lamps and spark radio transmitters, any ship leaving port on any voyage went out of sight of land and virtually disappeared. The only possible news would be a sighting and exchange of flag signals with another vessel about to make port. It was a duty to make such a report, a 'shipping intelligence' as it was called, and from these reports, Lloyds made up their famous list.

Short sea passages rarely took a ship out of contact for long. In low visibility it might be for a few hours, but Highland Railway steamers on their route to Portree were not normally out of touch for more than an hour during the crossing of Inner Sound. Fog is very rare on the windy coasts of Wester Ross and on this September night, as *Ferret* left Loch Carron, the visibility was several miles despite the wind and rain. Her oil masthead lamps were clearly seen.

But as soon as darkness fell completely, *Ferret's* lamps were extinguished and she turned south then southeast, past tiny Black Isle to glide through the narrow Sound of Sleat only half a mile from Kyle of Lochalsh which, until the railway came in 1897, was a mere fishing hamlet. She steamed at full speed out into the wider waters of the Western Isles and clear into the Atlantic, passing down the western side of Ireland.

The Company's employees, with waiting friends and relatives, on the quay at Portree were not unduly worried when the ship, often a little late, had not arrived at eleven o'clock. By midnight they were anxious. They waited all night and the ship never came. A search by every possible boat began soon after dawn, but to no avail. It had to be assumed *Ferret* was lost without trace.

There was equal consternation on board but the

passengers found themselves powerless, virtually pris-
oners of a Captain Watt none knew from previous cross-
ings, and by powerful officers called Wright and Walker.
There was also a man who claimed he was a 'Mr Smith',
related to the First Lord of the Admiralty. No information
was given to the unfortunate Portree-bound passengers
but at first they were adequately fed and able to use the
primitive berths, each with a rough blanket and pillow.
Rumours were rife that they were going to Marseilles
and would be put ashore in Gibraltar. Others said the
destination was to be Rio de Janeiro! Clearly the rich
cargo of whisky and good Scots pine was a major factor.

Sails were raised on the masts by the small crew who
had clearly obtained some practice, probably on the run
to Cardiff the trip before. Atlantic winds, followed later
by the Portuguese Trade Winds, moved *Ferret* through
the water with little coal necessary to keep her going at a
good ten knots.

Apparently, the passengers, some of whom were
regular Skye trippers, did not know the crew apart from a
frightened messman. It is not known how they passed
their time, or what degree of sea-sickness they suffered as
the small ship pitched and rolled in an Atlantic swell. No
storms threatened her, however, and on the eighth day
she came in sight of a very mountainous island. The
anchor was dropped in a sheltered bay, and the port
lifeboat lowered. It was often the practice in Western Isles
trading to use boats to reach shores without adequate
piers, and the ship's boats always had good capacity. All
seventeen people from the train were out in the boat and
rowed ashore by a couple of crewmen, who promptly
returned to the *Ferret*.

The castaways were told that they had been landed 'on
one of the Canary Islands and would soon be home'. It
was, in fact, La Palma, remote by todays standards and
even more remote in the 1880s. They saw the Highland
Railway steamer, her name painted out and *India* substi-

tuted on the bows and stern, up-anchor and steam away, unfurling her sails to obtain the benefit of the Trade Winds.

Somewhere in the Atlantic four days prior to reaching La Palma, the crew had thrown overboard a piece of simulated wreckage bearing the name *Ferret*. This was washed up on the Spanish coast and when eventually reported by cable to Lloyds it was assumed the ship had been lost in a storm, although the famous insurers, and the Highland Railway officers, were deeply puzzled as to how the traces had reached Spain when they had believed *Ferret* must have turned turtle somewhere in the middle of the Inner Sound.

Meanwhile the marooned railway passengers on La Palma had encountered fishermen, but communication between them was hopeless. No passengers had any knowledge of Spanish, although they were efficient in Gealic, and the fishermen knew no English. But they were fed and wined (or watered if teetotal as a few of the 'Wee Frees' undoubtedly were) and later escorted over rough tracks for weary hours to a small town.

It took days for the situation to be clarified, and even then little could be done for La Palma was not then connected to the cable network. Eventually they were taken by fishing boat on a two day journey to the big island of Tenerife, where at Santa Cruz contact was made with the British Consul.

At last the Highland Railway at Inverness and Lloyds of London knew what had happened to the *Ferret*. But by that time the stolen ship had coaled in the Cape Verde Islands and continued on a southerly course. There were few formalities in coaling in those days, payment being by cash and the British Golden Sovereign a welcome coin (one of them bought over two tons of fuel).

As for the weary Portree passengers, it took weeks before passage was found for them as 'Distressed British Subjects' on a vessel bound for the Clyde. Once in Glasgow they were put on a train for Inverness where, it is believed the Highland Railway refunded their fares for the journey to Portree and sent them on their way again; this time the steamer passage from Strome Ferry was aboard the carefully checked *Carham*. They reached their destination about three months after first departing from Inverness on a September afternoon!

The Highland Railway described the incident as 'a theft of one of our ships'. Apparently it was not piracy, nor could it be described as barratry, and the expression 'hi-jack' was not heard until the Chicago gangster days of the 1920s. The Company never recovered *Ferret*, but it did sell her when she was discovered in - of all places - Melbourne, Australia. She had changed her name before leaving the Cape Verdes with coal, and made the voyage around the Cape of Good Hope to take more coal in Durban under her new name, paying once more with golden coin. With a mixture of fuel economy and sails she 'ran her easting down' to Australia, as so many sailing ships of the time did, with the strong prevailing westerly winds behind her.

*Ferret* came to Port Phillip Bay as *India* and her stolen cargo of whisky was sold, but attempts to sell the ship failed. Lloyds had no record of a ship called *India* of that tonnage and description, resulting in the whole criminal business being exposed. Curiously, the crew were discharged by the Australian Court and stayed in that country, but Smith and Walker got seven years hard labour, and Wright was sentenced to forty-five months. Captain Watt appears to have been discharged with his First Mate and the rest of the crew. This was in 1881, in late September.

According to H A Vallance's *Highland Railway* history, the railway company sold the ship on the spot to the Adelaide Steamship Company for whom she worked on the Adelaide-Port Lincoln run for nearly forty years, eventually being wrecked on the Yorke Peninsula in 1920.

# 4

# 'Nuggets from Golden Arrow Days'

IT was the Chemin de Fer du Nord in France which started the luxury all-Pullman service between Paris and London under the title *Fleche d'Or (Golden Arrow)*. This happened on 11 September 1926 with a run from Paris Nord to Calais Maritime. Matching it on the English side of the Channel was an all-Pullman unnamed train from Dover Marine to Victoria.

Three years later the Southern Railway Company had built a fast turbine steamer named *Canterbury*, capable of making the Dover-Calais run in an hour (several times during its career this 28 knot ship recorded berth to berth times in fifty-five minutes). It was only then that the British Pullman train began to use the French title - in English - and the whole service became comprehensively luxurious, the upper deck lounge of *Canterbury* having Pullman-type seats and tables which were numbered to fit in with those passengers occupied on the two trains.

Boarding and disembarking were competently and speedily handled in those days, as befitted a service carrying commercially important, and sometimes Very Important, people. A flying bridge from the station platforms to the ship's upper deck was for *Golden Arrow* passengers' exclusive use. There was none of the post-war nonsense of curving queues and narrow gateways. Heavy luggage was handled swiftly and out of sight. Customs on the French side was conducted on board the train.

The *Golden Arrow* became the pride and joy of both the Southern and the Nord, carrying the cream of travellers between the two capitals, and looked set to continue that way. It was six hours to Paris with elegant snacks on the English train, and either a three-course standard lunch on board ship, if *Canterbury's* express speed and notorious motion permitted, or a lavish but rather late French lunch after leaving Calais.

But even the best laid plans can go awry. The year 1932 brought an unexpected shock. Four ungainly giant biplanes, known as Handley Page 42s, had been built in 1931 (plus four more which went to the Middle East) carrying names like *Heracles* and *Hannibal*. Each seated thirty eight passengers in a large measure of comfort. These passengers were served high quality meals by stewards during the two and a half hour flight to Paris. Another mineral, silver, was a prefix for the lunch and dinner flights, *Silver Wing*.

By the end of 1932, figures showed that Imperial Airways had carried more passengers between London and Paris than the *Golden Arrow*. The top of the market fell away. Second class passengers were admitted to the trains on both sides of the Channel, but never third class in France even up to 1971 when the service finished. The English Pullmans were, in fact, marked 'Third Class' but Boat Trains had a fare structure which included 'Second' (rarely seen elsewhere in the 1920s and 1930s in Britain). In France, second class passengers rode in ordinary coaches.

Thanks to various alternative routes on the Southern Railway out of Victoria, the *Golden Arrow* could always be diverted if tracks were blocked. It had an enviable record for timekeeping and avoiding problems.

Periodically in the winter arrangements of both pre-war and post-war days the train was routed to Folkestone, which enabled the French to use only one train for the service where loads were lighter. It ran from Paris Nord to Boulogne.

It was on a winter Friday in 1937 when the English Pullmans were ready to leave Folkestone Harbour, and the heavy train was about to be hauled up the steep gradient to the Junction at the top of the Leas cliffs by two small tank locomotives, aided by one pushing from the rear. The start was slow and across the viaduct speed reached about ten miles an hour, when passengers in a Pullman coupe at one end of the luxurious car were horrified to see the feet of a man outside their window. The feet disappeared when they called the attendant urgently. He could see nothing untoward from the window but from the corridor he heard cries and along-side the barely moving train, biting into the 1 in 28 climb, a Southern Railway timekeeper, Mr James Wilson, was running to keep up, shouting and waving.

The *Golden Arrow* was brought to an abrupt halt. Between two pullmans, hanging upside down, his head bumping the sleepers, was Mr Julian Bray, a passenger from Boulogne on his way home to his substantial Albury Lodge in Broxbourne, Hertfordshire. Mr Bray had leapt for the train as it departed, clutched a side-rail by a Pullman door, and somehow swung upside down between two car ends. Apart from a few cuts to his head and bruises to his legs, he was not seriously hurt, and after first aid was given aboard the delayed train, he was able to continue his ride home! Had it been a start from Dover Marine with faster acceleration, he would scarcely have survived.

The *Golden Arrow* was carefully laid-up during World War II but restarted on 15 April 1946, the first luxury train to resume service. Curiously, it was less threatened by competition from aircraft than it had been fourteen years earlier, and ran with full and satisfied loads until British European Airways got its act together in 1952 with a resumption of *Silver Wing* flights in Elizabethan-type aeroplanes taking ninety minutes from Northolt to Paris (Le Bourget).

A smart bar-car called the *Trianon* was a great attraction on the English train from 1946 onwards, but the French train began to lose its Pullmans (some had been damaged or destroyed during the War). Often it was down to two, and later to just one, usually the second unit of rolling stock behind the always clean and elegant 'Pacific' which hauled it from Amiens to Calais.

By 1960 the English train was beginning to show signs of wear. Or so it seemed to passengers returning from France in the late afternoon of a November day that year. Steam was still in charge of the haul, but this was to be replaced by electric engines (with *Golden Arrow* headboards) the next year. A Bulleid 'Battle of Britain' class Pacific was tackling its load vigorously and had passed Ashford on time at 70mph, accelerating to 75 by the time Headcorn was passed. Then, suddenly, the brakes came on hard and the train ground to a halt short of Staplehurst. There it stayed, stuck, with the locomotive simmering, as the crew diagnosed a hot box on the Pullman.

It was a long wait. Traffic backed up to Ashford and beyond. Eventually, the *Arrow* moved, slowly at first then faster, passing Paddock Wood but slowing again, with a curious exhaust beat from the Bulleid Pacific. Progress was erratic towards Tonbridge, where the train came to a complete stop and the engine departed. Interested passengers learned later that the regulator had jammed and the driver was operating on the cut-off for the last seven miles.

The long stop at Tonbridge gave the opportunity to pull the train apart, remove the Pullman with the troublesome box (hot again) and put on another locomotive.

Fortunately, Tonbridge had a 'King Arthur' on hand and this splendid veteran took over.

A year before electrification and two years before the final demise of the 'King Arthurs', passengers and platform spectators along the thirty miles to Victoria were treated to one of these grand old 4-6-0s in full cry, just like the 1930s when they often tackled the *Golden Arrow*. It was even time to Victoria, but the final last run was not appreciated by a majority of passengers to whom a London arrival two hours late was a poor return for the extra fare.

# 5

# The Freight Train That Waited at Harwich

SOME light rain and mist dimmed the visibility at Parkeston Quay in Essex on the morning of 27 October 1908 but it was quite mild and the busy Great Eastern Railway packet-port was fully active. The overnight express ship from the Hook of Holland had come in on time, and her two boat trains sent swiftly on their way, one to Liverpool Street, the other to Lincoln and the north.

As the day wore on, a day boat with passengers to the Hook of Holland departed and the little Danish passenger vessel from Esbjerg arrived at noon. A J15 0-6-0 of a Great Eastern type which served the region for well over half a century began to back her train load of flat wagons across the main lines and onto the quay.

The goods train was in position to accept its load from the steamer *Yarmouth*, coming from the Hook with fresh meat in its deck and hold containers. The engine was detached and proceeded to the yards for some temporary duties, ready to take up her train again for an anticipated evening departure.

At 10.30 that morning, the neat little twin-screw steel cargo ship *Yarmouth*, of 805 gross tons, cast off from the Hook of Holland bound for Parkeston Quay. Built by

31

Earle's of Hull in 1901, she was one of three sister ships serving the Great Eastern Railway's cargo services to Holland and Belgium. *Yarmouth* had made this day crossing at an average speed of 14 knots, relatively fast for the period, more than 200 times, as had her sisters *Ely* and *Newmarket* from Antwerp and Rotterdam.

*Yarmouth* had a load of 443 tons of meat, some of it stacked in wrapped bundles around the deck containers. There were in fact 192 tons of carcass meat which were not containerised, because some containers were loaded with furniture.

In addition to her crew of twenty-one men, headed by Captain Arthur Avis, *Yarmouth* was carrying one passenger, although she was not equipped with passenger accommodation. He was a butcher from Dovercourt near Harwich, and a brother of the ship's second engineer.

Very few ships were fitted with wireless in 1908, and it was not mandatory for cargo vessels but some passenger liners including those on the Hook express route, and a few lightships, had early spark transmitters. There was such an instrument aboard the Outer Gabbard Light, which *Yarmouth* passed close to, right on schedule at 5.30pm, as dusk was settling over the calm sea. It was misty and some drizzle had fallen but the crews exchanged waves. Although visibility was down to two miles, the lightshipmen reported that *Yarmouth* was going well. They noticed she took one or two fairly heavy rolls as she altered course at full speed.

The lightship called Parkeston Quay as a matter of routine, the sparks barking out that *Yarmouth* was on time and would pass the Sunk Light in less than an hour. This was the signal for railwaymen at the quay to summon loaders to the cargo berth in preparation, and to alert the assigned J15 locomotive to prepare for her goods train. In less than two hours, *Yarmouth* would be docking and the meat required speedy handling.

Less than an hour from Parkeston Quay, at 14 knots, the Sunk Lightship was lit and *Yarmouth* was sighted coming up close. In fact she was so close that shouted greetings were exchanged in the darkness, the lightship skipper having used his night-glasses to confirm the identity of the small cargo vessel. The Sunk made a routine report to the Great Eastern Railway's primitive radio station at the quay as *Yarmouth* made the course alteration necessary to take her past the Cork Light, five miles distant and the last one on the way to the mouth of the combined Stour and Orwell rivers on the North bank of which the modern port of Felixstowe (then a tiny place with a holiday resort attached) is situated.

But *Yarmouth* never reached the Cork light. She was never seen again. No physical trace of her, was ever found.

Back at Parkeston Quay, all was in readiness for her arrival, the freight locomotive panting at the head of its train, the distinctive Great Eastern Westinghouse brake wheezing. It was dark and very misty, a gloom which permitted perhaps a mile of visibility. Her arrival time came and went, but the delay occasioned no anxiety since it was assumed she was going very slowly on the up-river approach. The Hook of Holland day-boat had arrived and was disgorging passengers and mail, but that was a 20 knot vessel and normally overtook the freighter. The 'Hookers' officers had not seen *Yarmouth* but in the misty conditions they would not have expected to. Someone sent word to the cargo quay that *Yarmouth* had anchored in the estuary to await clearer conditions, and this resulted in the J15 locomotive and her crew (who worked a ten hour shift in those days) being sent off for other duties.

Next morning, however, as dawn came up slowly and reluctantly out of a misty east, the ship had still not arrived and it was clear that she had not anchored on the approaches to Harwich Harbour. The train of flat wagons still stood alongside the empty berth at the Quay.

Well before noon a number of people had gathered beside the freight train, including relatives and friends of the crew of *Yarmouth*. There was no fresh news, and telegrams confirmed that she had not put back to the Hook nor entered any other port. Officials despatched the relief Hook of Holland steamer *Vienna* from her moorings off the quay (ships on the express routes to the Hook and to Antwerp worked two weeks on and one week off) to search for the missing cargo ship.

Shortly after *Vienna* sailed, the Navy Commander-in-Chief at the Nore sent His Majesty's cruiser *Blake* from Sheerness to help in the search. Both these ships had wireless and kept the station at Parkeston Quay fully informed of what they were doing. The weather had cleared and it was bright and sunny during the afternoon but a mist came down at sunset.

Gloom at the quay was suddenly dispelled, however, as a report came in that *Yarmouth* was at last coming round Beach End buoy off Felixstowe and would be entering that harbour within minutes. Hopes ran high as a little steamer came out of the misty autumnal twilight and moved slowly up the Stour to the quay. But the hopes and expectations were mercilessly crushed as her name became visible; she was the *Newmarket*, an identical ship on the cargo run from Rotterdam.

Again a J15 goods locomotive was summoned and came to the berth to head up the empty wagons which had stood on the line for twenty four hours. This time containers were loaded on to them, and by 10pm the train was on its way up the line towards Manningtree. Ominously the authorities did not provide any more wagons for the cargo no longer expected from *Yarmouth*.

An official announcement was not made until 3.30pm on the afternoon of 29 October, when Great Eastern Railway officials at Liverpool Street (Headquarters of the railway system) said:- 'There is no longer any doubt that the cargo steamer *Yarmouth* has foundered. Little hope remains of any survivors being picked up. HMS *Blake* has recovered the body of fireman Bert Wright in a lifebuoy marked *Yarmouth, Harwich,* and also a furniture van.'

Captain Smy in *Vienna* located some more lifebuoys and a container of meat. Three days later the body of Fred Warner, another of *Yarmouth's* firemen, was washed up on the beach below the crumbling cliffs of the Suffolk village of Dunwich.

Remarkably, a few days later, a container was also washed ashore at Dunwich, and this was found to have live pigs in it. These pigs were, in fact, the only living things recovered from the lost vessel. To this day no one can be certain of what happened to this well-found, twin-screw steamer on a regular run only a dozen miles from her berth on a calm evening.

All East Anglia was shocked for it was the second disaster to a Great Eastern steamer within a year, the Hook express ship *Berlin* having been wrecked with considerable loss of life on the breakwater at the Hook in 1907. The Mayor of Harwich set up a relief fund for the relatives which was well subscribed.

A year later a greater mystery of the sea occurred in South African waters when the liner *Waratah* disappeared without trace, and in the subsequent inquiry it was felt that a similar fate had overtaken her (but in heavy seas), in that she suddenly took a series of heavy rolls and capsized. In the case of the *Yarmouth* Inquiry the official view held that she was top heavy due to excessive loading, one on top of the other, of containers. This form of cargo handling, now so widespread, suffered a setback and was not actively employed at sea for another thirty years.

Freight trains at Parkeston Quay began to shed their flat wagons and made up with more conventional trucks. Until the greater disaster of World War I, the memories of the goods train that did not set out on the appointed night were kept alive in the shed and goods yard at Parkeston Quay.

Rather oddly, the case of the lost *Yarmouth* was never raised during a longer enquiry, seventy-eight years later, when *Spirit of Free Enterprise* capsized in full view of watchers on shore in Zeebrugge Harbour.

---

A MAN of the cloth was travelling with a non-clerical friend in a train passing along the Cambrian Coast some thirty years ago. Staring out of the window, enraptured by the scenery, the clergyman said he regretted that the train seemed to be going so fast.

'I would willingly pay ten pounds if we could stop here and look at these views for a bit longer,' he said to his friend. 'Right. Your wish is granted, at half price.' With that his friend got to his feet and pulled the communication cord.

# 6

# Valedictory Journey on the East Kent Light Railway

IN the days when the Kent coalfield was in its prime, a standard guage light railway served the small towns with pits and linked them to Shepherdswell on the Canterbury to Dover line of the former South Eastern and Chatham Railway.

Its 'main line' was 11¼ miles long, from Shepherdswell to Canterbury Road, Wingham, and there was a branch from Eastry near Sandwich to Sandwich Road, 2½ miles long, which passed through Poison Cross Halt. This branch had given up the ghost long before World War II, but the 'main line' continued to move miners going to and from their shifts and their wives going shopping until the early 1950s. With the post-war prosperity in the pits and the demand for coal, miners bought cars and their wives were catered for by improved bus services, while the coal winged its way to the coastal ports by overhead transporters.

The last days of the East Kent Light Railway began soon after nationalisation, when in common with many other lightly used branches and former private railways under the wings of the 'Big Four', closure was the objective of the new British Transport Commission. One recalls the utterances of the Government politicians of the period who claimed that 'The railways now belong to the people.' One of the first results of nationalisation was the shutting down of lines which had carried at least some of 'the people' cheaply.

But the East Kent, from 1948 onwards, could hardly claim to be carrying any of the people. Its halts were closed, its weak infrastructure with sidings tailing off into what were known locally as the 'boondocks' totally overcome by roads and aerial freightways. It did not even get a reasonable turnout on its last week of passenger working, probably because it was just short of the birth of genuine preservation movements.

On the last day but one, an enthusiast boarded the train at Sheperdswell. There was one elderly coach hauled by an 01 tank engine. He was the only passenger. Leisurely progress was made to the outskirts of Canterbury Road, where the engine went off to the goods yard. The guard then allowed the carriage to roll towards the station platform but it came to a stop. The guard called out:- 'You must get out - I'm not pushing you any further.' He duly walked to Canterbury Road, where a goods clerk was on duty. Asked how many passengers he booked, the reply was that he was the first that week.

# 7

# Trains That Did Not Stop ...

THOSE once familiar leaflets which used to hang outside the ticket windows of so many Southern Railway booking offices made it quite clear that Restalls were running excursions to Bognor Regis. We tore a buff-coloured Restalls leaflet from the billhook and found the price was right (six shillings and sixpence, $32\frac{1}{2}$p in the present currency), the timings were right (stopping to pick up at Norwood Junction at 9.45am and stopping to set down at 6.43pm, and the day (Wednesday) was right.

Exactly on time, which was not surprising since the train had started from London Bridge with a subsequent call at New Cross Gate, a B4X 4-4-0 hauled its heterogeneous collection of corridor and non-corridor green bogies into platform 4 at Norwood Junction.

It was 1937, a year before the Mid-Sussex line, now called the Arun Valley line, was electrified, although third rail existed to Dorking North and was rapidly being extended. We called at West Croydon, and then Sutton, following which came a relatively fast run to Horsham. Excursionists bound for Littlehampton duly changed at Ford Junction, while the whole train carried on to Bognor, stopping briefly at Barnham Junction.

It was a typical midweek Restalls bargain train oper-

ated over Southern Railway metals with reasonable efficiency, scarcely delayed by regular service traffic, and it
arrived in Bognor two hours after leaving London
Bridge. Passengers enjoyed their promised five hours
beside the sea and returned to the small terminus to find
their train ready for them and the same B4X in charge.

All went well to Horsham, where the engine took
water. But shortly after the guard flagged his train away
there was consternation among our party, and no doubt
among the comparatively few passengers who had a
working knowledge of Southern Railway lines, for we
took the right hand tracks and headed for Crawley and
Three Bridges. Wondering how the Sutton and West
Croydon excursionists would fare, we unhooked the
leather straps and pulled the windows down to watch
our somewhat hesitant progress along the line, slowing
to a crawl past Faygate signal box, to come to a definite
and quite lengthy stop at Crawley.

No one alighted and no officials made any announcements. The train went on to Three Bridges, halting briefly
before the junction with the main Brighton line. There
they called out, 'Next stop East Croydon; passengers for
Sutton change at Norwood Junction.'

Out of course, the Restall excursion took the Redhill
route from Three Bridges, reaching East Croydon in a
little over half an hour. The stop there was of several
minutes duration, with most if not all the West Croydon
passengers alighting. The locomotive topped up with
water from the hose at the end of platform 4.

The B4X accelerated its train on the $1\frac{3}{4}$ miles run to
Norwood Junction, showed no sign of slowing and ran
through the station at about 45mph. Our party's consternation turned to alarm. No doubt the Sutton passengers
gave up hope.

On the four track main line just beyond the Goathouse
Bridge, brakes were applied sharply and the train came
to a stop a little short of Anerley. As it was on the up fast

line, the station, which only had platforms serving the slow lines, was of little use. There was no question of setting back for a full mile on such a busy route.

Clearly some decision had been taken a few minutes later, for the locomotive accelerated her train swiftly away and ran for London Bridge, achieving well over 60mph on the descent from Honor Oak Park to New Cross Gate, only coming to a stop for signals a quarter of a mile short of the terminus.

Once into a platform, which turned out to be the South Eastern low level, it was only the first to alight who caught a glimpse of the driver and fireman, seen briefly in the company of officials hurrying them through the barrier as the B4X hissed at the buffers, deserted. But a Restalls man came along to see his excursionists through the barriers onto electric suburban trains for Norwood Junction and West Croydon.

This was not the first occasion I had been on a steam train which overshot Norwood Junction where it was due to stop. A 1₃ 4-4-2 tank hauling three coaches on an afternoon run from Oxted to London Bridge left East Croydon in determined style. Although in 1935 most steam trains on the Oxted line ran non-stop from East Croydon to Victoria or London Bridge, a few were scheduled to call at Clapham Junction or Norwood Junction, and the train I was on was one of them.

Speed must have been near to 50mph when the train reached the platform end, but at the northern end brakes were applied smartly and the short rake of coaches were brought to an abrupt stop short of the Goathouse Bridge. Without further ado, the driver began to set back, no doubt hoping he was still covered by the signals, and we came back into platform 3 less than a minute after thundering through it.

Stafford Woodhams, the formidable but much respected station master who had held the Norwood Junction post (also covering Anerley and Penge West), was a furious figure as he ran up from the subway and confronted the driver. Clearly he felt slighted that his station had been treated to a run past and expressed himself accordingly.

Grateful passengers left the train, however, and some watched and listened. The delay was not more than a minute before the handsome 1₃ tank was waved away for its eight and a half mile run to London Bridge.

Failure to stop or to take the correct route is not and was not a prerogative of the Southern Railway and its successor. Even a French TGV hurtled through Le Creusot in 1982 when due to stop and pick up a party of very important industrialists who had been doing business at a major factory in the town. It made no attempt to slow down but roared on out of sight, leaving the leader of the party to make difficult alternative transport arrangements for the return to Paris.

In the summer of 1975 the Mayor of Teignmouth and a group of resort dignitaries waited on the down platform of the South Devon town to greet several travel industry people coming from London on a special promotional visit. Newspaper photographers held their cameras at the ready as the yellow-fronted Western class diesel hydraulic appeared from the Dawlish tunnels.

It was the right train beyond doubt, and running to time. But it passed through Teignmouth doing at least 60mph, the wind of its passage causing two people to fall over backwards and the mayor to lose his hat.

In fact the express did not stop until Newton Abbot, nearly five miles away. Most of the travel industry people had been treated to considerable British Rail hospitality on the journey and probably did not realise they had just been to Teignmouth. The Western Region escort did, and one or two of the more knowledgable guests knew something had gone wrong, but nobody sought to have a 'free' pull on the alarm cord.

At Newton Abbot the driver insisted that nobody had

told him to stop at Teignmouth, where he had been some-what fearful of the closeness to the platform edge of 'a bunch of railway enthusiasts' trying to take pictures of the already doomed Western diesels. The VIP passengers were treated to some liquid refreshment at the buffet before joining a local service which took them back to Teignmouth in time for a rather late lunch at which the mayor expressed himself forcefully about the treatment of his town.

# 8

# Snow Comes to the Surrey Hills

THE winter of 1963, from the very beginning of January to the middle of March, was regarded as the second worst in England this century, beaten only by the prolonged horror of 1947. Train services suffered throughout the country, particularly on the Southern Region, where snow-covered or iced conductor rails were a serious problem.

One day in late January, at Sutton station, a passenger waiting to travel up the branch to Epsom Downs observed trains sliding down the line, having been stabled at Epsom Downs and able to get out on the track for the four mile trip to Sutton. No train had attempted to go the other way.

After a lengthy wait an electric arrived at platform 4, and the station master appeared, enquiring from the motorman what train he was. The reply was that he 'didn't know' since things were so disorganised but that he hoped to go up to Epsom Downs. The station master told him to terminate at Sutton and go to London Bridge. Passengers on the up platform were instructed to join this train.

Before departure, however, the station master appeared again and told him that he was going to Epsom

Downs with steam assistance. The London-bound passengers were evacuated onto the icy platform and told to go over to the up line where some train or other would soon collect them.

Presently a local freight from Hackbridge came came steaming in behind a C2X 0-6-0 which detached from its few wagons in a siding and after much shunting, backed on to the electric. It was duly coupled to the front end and soon pulled away smartly, the electric taking power with an incredible display of flashing from the conductor rail. The heavy goods steam engine made light work of the gradient and the snow covered track, made the stops at Belmont and Banstead, and arrived at Epsom Downs within ten minutes.

The locomotive stayed on the electric for the return trip to Sutton, detached, and pushed the next electric uphill to Epsom Downs, where it spent a useful half an hour shunting backwards and forwards crunching snow and clearing the then extensive sidings. Finally, it hauled an electric down to Sutton and collected its own freight wagons. One young man who was a passenger that day become a regional general manager with BR. When asked what was his favourite engine he dug out many photographs and replied 'C2X with double domes and clench bracket'.

# 9

# Severn Tunnel Sanctuary

IN October 1940 the war was going badly for Britain, with the Blitz on London gathering force despite the September victories in the air, and the Army, recovered from the Beaches of Dunkirk, as yet not re-armed. But the services and style of the railway companies were still at pre-war standards apart from schedules and frequencies.

On the Great Western, no trains left Paddington for Cardiff and Swansea between the 1.55pm and the 5.55pm. Returning from a bomb-disturbed leave to my ship at Barry Island awaiting the assembly of a North Atlantic convoy to be formed at Milford Haven, I travelled by the 5.55pm on a late October evening. This train, made up to seventeen coaches still including first and third class dining cars, was hauled by *Tregenna Castle*, and a creditable run of forty-five minutes brought us to Reading. Swindon was reached at 7.35pm, exactly on time by the slower austerity schedule.

Having taken a ticket for second dinner, I was called to the first class diner shortly before we stopped at the famous railway town. My status as a very junior officer entitled me to a first class warrant for up to three leaves a year (and I was returning from my first one), and the ambience of the diner was very appealing contrasted with the stark Mess Room aboard ship which had been, and would be again, the place to snatch meals on a stormy Atlantic for eighteen to twenty days at a stretch.

The menu, not yet severely affected by rationing, had a number of choices and cost three shillings and sixpence (17½p). A bottle of beer, served before the chosen soup, was 9d (4p). I knew that these prices were higher than in the third class, where a restricted dinner menu was priced at half a crown (12½p) and beer cost 8d (3½p) but we had more comfortable and spacious seats.

Blackout material covered the windows across which the curtains were drawn, allowing full lighting in the diner. Many fellow diners wore uniform, most of them senior to me.

As we left Swindon, my beer arrived. There were still plenty of waiters and the Great Western tradition was maintained. There was even 'deep apple tart prepared on board the train' to look forward to later.

We stopped at Badminton shortly after 8pm, but if any passengers boarded they did not clump through the diners with their luggage - a familiar occurrence later in the war until restaurant cars disappeared.

The train had gone through a station which I reckoned to be Winterbourne, running at close to the wartime maximum permitted, which was 65mph, when *Tregenna Castle* began to accelerate, her exhaust audible in the diner as it rose to a crescendo. Although there were no means of timing the train in the black-out, wheel clicks and the general motion convinced me we had gone beyond 75 and were perhaps approaching 80mph.

Suddenly the chief steward yelled from the end of the car 'Everyone get down on the floor or under the tables'. Two loud crumps were heard on the southern side of the express, then the lights were put out. An Army Officer opposite drew the curtains and lifted the blackout as we all crouched low. A vivid glow in the sky over Bristol showed that the city was under bomb attack, and so was the train

*Tregenna Castle* raced into the night, hurtling down the

1 in 90, and then 1 in 68, the heavy train quite certainly doing 85mph, perhaps slightly more. A noise louder than the train sounded from above, quickly followed by staccato bursts. There was a Nazi plane machine-gunning the fast moving express. A brief tunnel enveloped us and the speed increased still more. The noises from above ceased during our short transit and as we roared out into the open darkness again, lit up by the fires of nearby Bristol, the train had momentarily lost its attacker.

But the plane came back, loosed a bomb which exploded near to the track on the north side, and then opened fire with machine guns again, probably at the locomotive. Fortunately the Great Western tracks were still magnificent in 1940 and allowed the high speed - which must have been close to 90mph - without throwing the coaches about, nor even smashing dishes in the diner.

Into the Severn Tunnel we thundered and then the brakes were applied, bringing us to a comparatively smooth stop within two miles. There, deep under the river, we sought sanctuary. Voices were heard on the track and torches flashed here and there. One or two senior officer passengers opened the doors. We were told there was no serious damage and no casualties although the locomotive had been hit several times by bullets and the roof of the first coach was splintered. We stayed in the tunnel for half an hour, and in the diner we finished our meal in quiet safety. Resuming the journey we reached Newport only twenty-two minutes late.

# 10

# Incident on the Putney Loop

DURING the early 1960s many steam excursions were run, especially for railway enthusiasts, on the tracks of the Southern's southwestern section. One of these on a Sunday was returning from an outing to Salisbury and Yeovil, bound for stations on the eastern section.

The route lay via Wimbledon and East Putney to enable the train to reach the low level lines at Battersea. Approaching the junction at East Putney the driver made a full brake application, but before this could bring the train to a stop it had gone through the District Line platforms aiming for Putney Bridge.

It seems the East Putney box should have been kept open for this special Sunday evening occasion, but was not, in fact, manned. Wimbledon Park had offered the train ostensibly to East Putney, but the bell signal had gone through to Putney Bridge, where the signalman had accepted it, not recognising that the bell code was wrong.

A long delay followed while permission was laboriously obtained to set back eventually to the junction and a relief signalman found to open up and man the empty box. Fortunately this was a steam train headed by a Bulleid Pacific; had it been an electric it would have more than bridged the dead section on the bridge and would inevitably have connected the voltage of the southern to the different voltage system on London Transport, with results which could well have been disastrous.

Some passengers aboard the train were unhappy about the delay but a slight majority felt that it was worth it to undergo a most unexpected experience.

---

A POLISH visitor to England arrived at Dover from the Ostend ferry a few years ago and boarded the boat train for Victoria. He prided himself that he had learned English to perfection, having studied Shakespeare and watched numerous plays written by the Bard and performed in Warsaw in what he deeply believed was pure English.

His train, in the manner of many at Dover Marine which have missed their path due to the late arrival of a ferry, stayed at the platform. Witnesses swear to the story that he looked frequently at his watch, then slid open the top of the window to call at a nearby porter. 'Man, dallyest thou here long?'

# 11

# The Train from Liverpool is 'Lost'

THE evening of Saturday, 21 December was clear and mild in Liverpool as the 5.25pm restaurant car express stood at Lime Street Station awaiting departure for Euston. At the head of the train stood LMS Pacific No 6202, the unnamed turbine engine, a regular on this service and able to take the twelve coach train with ease on a recently improved schedule of three hours, thirty-five minutes.

I boarded this train at 5.15pm bound for Christmas leave from my ship, which had arrived in Liverpool the day before. It was pleasing to note that we got away in good style, accelerating up to Wavertree and maintaining speed through thickening mist at Runcorn.

The first dinner was announced and I took this without delay, anticipating a welcome home supper later that night. The fare was adequate, costing three shillings (15p) but rationing still held Britain in a tight grip eighteen months after the end of the war in Europe. Eating the meat course, which as usual in those days was heavily supported by vegetables, Crewe came and went, almost exactly on time.

Returning to my compartment well before Stafford, I dozed off for a while, awakening to find the train stopped in what seemed like almost total darkness. Looking out of the top part of the window I could see nothing, no lights apart from a red showing through the misty blackness ahead. It was about half past eight in the evening.

It was not easy to tell where we were. No trains passed in the other direction. Obviously, all hope of an on-time arrival had been abandoned. After half an hour I went in search of information. The guard said we were stopped 'somewhere near Lichfield but we hadn't got there yet'.

The train spent a frustrating three hours stationary, during which time no traffic of any kind went past. Then towards midnight it began to move, slowly at first but then gathering speed to run through Lichfield, Tamworth and Nuneaton, to come to a halt outside Rugby. Halt scarcely describes the situation, for the train just lay there, the engine not making the simmering sounds normally associated with a Pacific due to its experimental nature. But we passengers knew there was nothing wrong with 6202 - for no other trains passed us all this while.

A foray into the dining car, still lit and with tired stewards dozing in seats, yielded a pot of tea and a few biscuits. The second sitting had consumed all the more sustaining food. But it was better than nothing, especially when a few morsels of cheese were found.

Eventually, at nearly two o'clock in the morning, the train began moving again, and passed through Rugby and junctioned off to the left! We were taking the Northampton route. There was no explanation, and the guard, questioned frequently, came up with the answer:- 'We're lost'. At this time, it seems, people at Euston and those telephoning enquiries were told:- 'The 5.25pm from Liverpool has been lost track of…'

A stop for water at Northampton Castle station which we made about 2.45am may have furnished information as to our whereabouts. It was quite foggy but not densely so. Running on to Euston, the turbine locomotive did comparatively well, dashing through the murky London suburbs with only a few lights showing through the gloom to tell us we were nearing journey's end. This came with a good approach into Euston and at final stop at ten past four in the morning, some seven hours late!

The Great Hall was packed with people. There were no seats and even the marble floor was packed with luggage and kitbags. Under Hawkshaw's beautiful roof, thousands groaned and sat or stood, with nowhere to go until Sunday morning's tubes, trains and buses began their schedules. There was news of severely delayed or missing trains posted periodically on notice boards. No one said or knew what the cause of the trouble was, and I can only surmise a derailment of some kind blocking all tracks, probably south of Rugby. But no accident had been discovered for the night of 21 December 1946.

On the noticeboard was news of the 5.25pm from Liverpool. 'This train, due at 9pm, arrived at 4.10am after being reported misplaced'. None of the LMS top brass was about, but a very irate passenger off the train spotted what seemed to be a senior uniformed member of the Company's staff. He protested, demanded a taxi home, and some refreshments, none of which were supplied.'But we are eight hours late,' he shouted. 'No Sir, you are only seven hours late,' countered the official.

# 12

# 'Where Are You Going?'

REDHILL has been a difficult station for 150 years, and trains stopping there even today seem reluctant to get going again. Regular passengers heading for the coast or for Gatwick Airport (with planes to catch) are always at their ease when the train takes the Quarry-avoiding route.

One summer Saturday towards the end of steam operations, when the Guildford to Redhill and Redhill to Tonbridge lines were regularly worked by steam and through trains for the coast from the Midlands and north west were steam-hauled to their destinations over the electrified lines, a Southern Mogul brought in a heavy train from the Guildford-Reigate direction. The coaches bore headboards which read 'Birkenhead, Wolverhampton, Birmingham, Ramsgate, Margate'.

An announcement was made that the 'next train on platform 1 will be for Brighton, Eastbourne and Hastings'. The Mogul detached from the train, facing towards London, while another locomotive came off Redhill Shed with the Brighton headcode. This backed on to the train, while the signalman set the road for Horley and the South.

The guard, looking somewhat worried, came up to the engine. 'where are you going?' he demanded of the driver. 'Brighton', replied that worthy. 'Oh no you're not', said the guard. 'We are going to Margate'. The driver climbed from his cab and made his way to a telephone, closely followed by the alarmed guard. The fireman got down and uncoupled his locomotive. The driver returned, and without a word climbed into his cab and set off back to the shed.

The rake of coaches stood there at platform 1, silently, apart from irate passengers wanting to know what was happening. Word got around that the headboards were wrong. Apparently the train had arrived out of path and Control had not informed Redhill.

Eventually, the Mogul which had brought them in shunted around the train, with delays to all traffic, and took up station ready to cross all tracks again and take its train on the Tonbridge line. A departure for Brighton had been avoided by seconds.

# 13

---

# Elephant in Decay

---

FOR more than a century a fairly large goods yard served Kingston-upon-Thames, close to the station on the Surrey side of the river. Inevitably it fell into decline when British Railways threw away its small freight business, and the British Railways Property Board sold it to a housing developer in the early 1970s.

Half a dozen substantial houses were completed on the site and had been occupied when three of them started to sink. This was no ordinary subsidence - they began to accelerate downwards at the rate of several inches a day and needed to be abandoned in quite a hurry. As the structures collapsed and the roofs fell in an investigation was rapidly begun, with the hope of saving the three secure ones and others yet to be completed.

Was it something to do with an underground spring from the nearby Thames? Had there been some mining in the distant past? Why had the railway tracks survived for so long? These questions were considered with some urgency.

Investigations revealed a most curious historical event of some forty years in the past. A circus train had been accommodated in the goods yard and during the night a huge Indian elephant had died in its wagon. In the small hours of the morning a team of circus workers had dug a massive grave for the unfortunate beast on the waste ground to the side of the tracks. Next day, with an engine coupled to the train, the circus had 'folded its tents and stole away' without disclosing its loss.

In due time - as those of us who have come across dead elephants in East Africa know only too well - foul gases bloated the carcass and it eventually disintegrated under the ground, leaving a vast empty space into which the three houses sank so many years later! The Locomotive Club of Great Britain helped to explain the bizarre story.

# 14

# Sedgefield Shocker

ON a cold grey winter's morning early in 1929 a young man arrived at Sedgefield station in County Durham to take up his first railway duties as a porter. He was, in fact, a well educated lad from a good school and family. He had been accepted as a traffic apprentice by the London and North Eastern Railway, and to advance up the management grades required practical experience at all levels.

Sedgefield in those days was a comparatively small, neat station on the Middlesbrough to Ferryhill line, much used by coal traffic, but seeing only five passenger trains each way. Small tank engines coped with much of the passenger workings but hefty 0-8-0 former North Eastern Railway goods locomotives hauled heavy freights through the station, occasionally stopping there, while pick-up goods in the charge of ex-North Eastern 0-6-0s usually called at the platforms.

In the days of adequate staffing, there was still a good deal of work to do, and the young man whose name was Hughes laboured under the directions of the station master. About midday, he sat down on one of the platform seats during a lull in traffic and opened the traditional tin box he had been given, taking out his sandwiches.

He had just eaten the first one when a grizzled platelayer made his way from the tracks in the direction of Stillington, carrying a large parcel wrapped in newspaper. He came up the platform slope and made his way to the young porter. 'Found this on the line. What do you want to do with it?'

He unwrapped the folds of newspaper, revealing a human head!

Young Hughes lost his sandwich in a sudden upheaval, and his first day's lunchbox remained uneaten.

Suicides are not, sadly, very rare on rail tracks. This one was by a young unemployed man, known to have been severely depressed. His body, found later, had been flung into deep undergrowth some yards away.

# 15

# The Bull
# and the Royal Flowers

IN the days of the London and North Eastern Railway,
the 1.20pm form Kings'Cross to Edinburgh was always
a very popular and heavily loaded train. Its Gresley A3
Pacific always had to struggle with seventeen or eighteen
coaches to reach Grantham by 3.14pm although the
schedule eased somewhat as it progressed northwards,
being due at Newcastle at 6.29pm and Edinburgh at
8.45pm. Records show that for the full year 1937-38 it
averaged ten minutes late into Grantham but only two
minutes late into the Scottish capital.

One August day in 1937 a mass of fresh flowers were
loaded at King's Cross to decorate Holyrood House,.
where the King and Queen were coming the next day.
Just why London flowers had to be taken to Scotland for
the occasion has never been made clear, but the consign-
ment was rated high priority and carefully stored in
water containers in the first luggage van behind the locomotive.

A second luggage van was provided on this particular
run, with baggage piled high and - in a partitioned
section - a young bull, also bound for Scotland. This valuable animal had been purchased at auction and may have
been intended to improve the already high standards of

Scottish beef cattle.

One of the two East Coast inspectors had been assigned to the journey in the light of the importance of the Royal Flowers. They often rode the *Flying Scotsman* or the *Coronation* in the days before the war, and kept a careful eye on the 1.20pm with its high revenue return.

All went well to York, where the heavy train pulled in almost exactly on time at 4.46pm. Checking the first luggage van the East Coast inspector satisfied himself that the flowers were as fresh as when they had been loaded, and next door the guard had made friends with the young bull, which was munching happily at provisions of hay.

Newcastle-on-Tyne was reached at 6.30pm and here the load was lightened as three coaches were detached to form the Bergen Line Boat train down to Tyne Commission Quay. Sometimes at busy periods this ran as a separate train from London to serve the ships *Venus* or *Vega* but in mid-week the 1.20pm had to bear the extra weight. The guard and the inspector checked the detachment of rolling stock, then the latter went to a dining car for an early dinner.

He never reached the sweet course. A distraught guard came running into the diner with bad news. The bull was loose.

They went forward through the corridors expecting to meet the animal anywhere along the way and to hear the cries of alarmed passengers. But it had not entered the passenger accommodation. Instead, it had gone into the first luggage van, where it made a remarkably fast job of eating the flowers!

It is quite likely that neither the King nor the Queen noticed the next day that Holyrood House was decorated with fresh Scottish blooms instead of slightly faded varieties of southern English flowers.

The guard on the 1.20pm had a tiring and responsible job, not always rewarding, as that particular one found at the LNERs 'flower enquiry' held at Newcastle. But he was indeed more fortunate than one on the same train two years earlier.

The heavy train changed its Pacific locomotive at Grantham during an eight minute stop, and then ran fast to Doncaster. Seen to go on to the platform at Grantham, the guard was not the man who waved away the train. Station staff did that and the driver, not wanting to lose more time, started away. A ticket inspector on board went in search of the guard but could not find him anywhere.

At the Doncaster stop he informed the locomotive crew, suggesting that the guard must have been left behind at Grantham. Meanwhile, he said he would take over for the run to York, but notified that station of the need for a replacement.

Arriving at York about fifteen minutes late, the driver got down and took his oil can to his engine. He had felt a hint of sluggishness during the run. Meanwhile, two officials and the new guard came up to the locomotive to report that no trace of the guard had been found at Grantham. They did not think he had been left behind.

The driver suddenly stiffened and went very pale. 'No, he came with us. There he is, poor chap.' With that he pointed to a very nasty mess of remains and torn uniform caught up among the Pacific's driving wheels.

# 16

# 'Right Away Bob'

HIGH in the Pennines the station of Garsdale is often swept by sudden storms, which even in the height of summer can be of chilling hail. Today it presents a scene of desolation, relieved only occasionally when some steam excursion stops and eager passengers climb down on to the surviving platform for pictures.

But it used to be called Hawes Junction, where a branch line to Northallerton, through Hawes town and Redmire, went off to the east. In the days of the Midland Railway it was busy, always with an engine steaming somewhere in its vicinity, the unusual turntable frequently in use at this highest junction in England.

On Christmas Eve in 1910 there were no less than five engines in steam on the main line, while yet another was simmering on the branch platform wearing North Eastern Railway livery. By high Pennine standards it was not cold but it was windy and wet, with bursts of rain sweeping across and visibility was poor. A dirty night, it was also very dark with only swinging oil lamps and the glow of cab fires to relieve the dark, except for pinpoints of sometimes green and sometimes red signal lights.

Trains thundered through, fast goods in succession and a southbound express passenger for St Pancras followed by a special section needed on this day, before the annual Christmas holiday feast. The light engines-in-waiting were required for banking duties, for the Midland had no heavier locomotives than 4-4-0s for its passenger trains, and single-heading on a gale-blown night was insufficient to guarantee a weighty train getting over Ais Gill Summit successfully.

Three of the light engines, coupled together, waited to return to Leeds, while the other two, also coupled, were going back to Carlisle for further banking duties. All signals on the main line showed green at about half past five in the morning; the signalman in charge was confident of giving the road to the Scotch Express from St Pancras to Carlisle, which was reported running ten minutes late. He expected the three Leeds engines to get away on the green for their southbound trip. But it was the two Carlisle engines which opened their throttles and started up the gradient northwards.

The stage had been set for what became known as the Hawes Junction disaster. When the express overtook them, it struck the tender of the rear light locomotive and derailed, causing a fierce fire as the gas-lit coaches blew up and incinerated twelve passengers.

Many other passengers were badly burned or injured in other ways. Three of the dead could not be identified and they rest in graves in Hawes churchyard among the bodies of some navvies who helped build the Settle and Carlisle Railway.

A searching inquiry assigned blame in various proportions, mainly upon Signalman Sutton of Hawes Box, but partly upon the drivers of the light engines for not seeing the overtaking express in time and accelerating.

However, another factor came into the picture that black and stormy night. With both directions showing green, a senior stationhand, waving his lamp in the wet darkness, shouted, 'Right Away, Bob.'

Heard by the leading light engine driver Bob Scott, his directive was acted on and he opened his throttle for Carlisle while Driver Bath in the second engine followed suit as they stormed northwards.

But the leading engine driver of the three Leeds engines to whom the stationhand had really aimed his shout did not hear. His name was Bob, too.

---

SHILDON, County Durham, in August 1975 saw the largest crowds ever known at any event since the 1953 Coronation. They exceeded the total at all first division football matches when the season opened some weeks later.

The event was, of course, 'Rail 150', celebrating the 1825 opening of the Stockton and Darlington Railway. A steam parade marked the real break-through of a return to this time-honoured traction on sections of British Railways. Aerial photographs confirmed to the most sceptical railway officials that enthusiasm was measured, not in small groups of men but in hundreds of thousands of people.

Every stand seat was taken, many double-booked, and the stands extended for 1,000 yds. In the fields people stood up to eighty deep, and even two miles away cars parked on farm land had to pay £2 (a large sum before hyper-inflation hit the country).

The vast crowds were so unexpected by the authorities that there was panic, and a detachment of army was hurriedly called in from Catterick Camp to control the situation. A tough Sergeant Major made the decisions on which ticket was valid in the stands, and protesting occupiers were put out to grass or in wagons on the other side of the tracks.

# 17

# Death Before Disaster

In the early summer of 1945, the *Aberdonian* steamed northwards from King's Cross on its leisurely wartime schedule, hauled by a Gresley V2 locomotive. But the tracks beyond Hatfield were apparently not ready for the train's 70mph progress down towards Welwyn Garden City (there was a wartime maximum of 65 to allow for less maintenance).

Perhaps it was not the speed but the condition of the wooden LNER (ex Great Northern) coach directly behind the tender. Just past Hatfield this coach derailed, breaking its coupling to the locomotive and going over on its side with the underframe on the ballast. Remarkably, the rest of the train, including sleepers and the restaurant car recently restored to the service, stayed on the track, but the weight of the train pushed the derailed coach along in a grinding fashion as it came to a stop. The woodwork smashed to splinters.

Rescuers running from Hatfield station and from the stalled *Aberdonian* found a dead body. There was no trace of any other, nor of injured passengers. They stared at the dead man, waxed and with hands linked together in repose. He had been dead long before the accident. The rescuers had found a corpse. They also found the empty coffin with smashed lid in which the body was being transported to Aberdeen.

# 18

# The Bomber and the Diner

THE sturdy but elegant splendour of a traditional Midland Railway dining car can still be seen at the National Railway Museum. The six-wheeled bogies and their Mansell oak fillings gave them a ride over the magnificent Midland main line which was so smooth that waiters filled Sherry glasses to the brim even when the train was travelling at more than 60mph.

The decorated ceilings and lavish clerestory shed a warm glow over the proceedings at mealtimes, both in first and third class. So it was on a Thursday in September 1936 when the 10.25am express from St Pancras to Manchester was travelling at a steady 60mph between Radlett and Napsbury on the London side of St Albans. It was too early for lunch but both classes of passengers were enjoying coffee and biscuits in their respective diners as the brand new Class 5 4-6-0 up front was accelerating into a run which scheduled Leicester as the first stop in 104 minutes (to be cut by five minutes in the great LMS speed-up the next year).

Suddenly the first class dining car was rocked by a heavy noise and darkness fell, as did the glass from the clerestory and lamps. An RAF bomber, belonging to No 214 (Bomber) squadron stationed at Scampton Aerodrome near Lincoln, its flaps down for a landing at the Handley Page Aerodrome, Radlett, had landed bang on the dining car instead.

Someone pulled the communication cord and the train slowed almost immediately, the plane sliding off the diner's roof and into an adjoining field. Once relieved of its unwelcome load, the train continued on to St Albans, where it stopped for a five minute examination. Mr E A Wager of Brentwood, the senior dining car attendant, reported that no one was injured in the damaged vehicle, the four seats directly under where the bomber's wheels struck were the only ones unoccupied. But splinters of wood and glass had flown everywhere, without hitting any passengers.

The express resumed its journey to Leicester with only one active diner, but at Leicester they coupled on a fresh first class car with kitchen attached. Overall, the train was seventeen minutes late into Manchester, but the bomber was a write-off; its two pilots miraculously escaped unhurt. Its undercarriage was retrieved from the diner at Leicester.

# 19

# Lightning Strikes Again

THE Great Western Railway was rightly proud of its safety record established over more than four decades. There had been a sad disaster on the system on 10 November 1890, when an up Ocean Liner special crashed into a goods train at Norton Fitzwarren, two miles from Taunton in Somerset. Ten passengers were killed due to a signalman's error at this junction.

By the year 1930, the Great Western could claim it had carried hundreds of millions of passengers without causing loss of life to a single one. There had been a few minor accidents such as engine derailments, and in a few cases company employees had been killed, but armed with Automatic Train Control and a special vigilance, the management looked forward to achieving fifty years without disaster.

On a warm afternoon in 1937, Mr (later Sir James) Milne, the General Manager, heard with horror the news of a bad derailment at Shrivenham on the line between Swindon and Didcot. An up express from Bristol had come off the line at speed, three coaches hurtling across the ballast and demolishing a platelayers hut. 'Three people killed,' he was told on the telephone. But shortly afterwards came news that the coaches had remained upright, that a few passengers had been slightly injured. The deaths were all track maintenance men, whose work had, in fact, caused the derailment by incomplete finishing.

It was generally put about in the 1930s that 'The safest place in the world was the interior of a British Railway carriage'. 'Particularly,' it was added, 'A Great Western one.' No major transport organisation in the world had such a good record of safety, and probably never will. The Railway Passengers Assurance Company in 1939 quoted the odds against being killed as a passenger on the Great Western as 'a thousand million to one' (we did not use the billion in those days except for a million-million). However, the unique Schwebebahn of Wuppertal in the Ruhr has carried 1,500,000,000 passengers without fatality since 1900.

The war imposed tremendous strains on the railways of Britain and the Blitz destroyed bridges, track and rolling stock, but the Great Western escaped severe attacks. In Chapter 9 we saw how one express, heading for Wales, escaped with only minimal damage. As November came in 1940, the Great Western management noted, without any public statement, that in a few days they would be able to claim 'Fifty Years without a Fatality.' Perhaps they forgot to touch the wood of Churchward's chair.

On a dirty black morning a couple of miles west of Taunton, the 9.50pm train to Plymouth, which had left Paddington on 3 November packed with nearly 1,000 passengers, crashed at Norton Fitzwarren. The train, more than an hour late due to Blitz problems in the London area, went through catch points just beyond the Somerset junction station and *King George VI* rolled over, dragging five coaches over with it. The cause was driver error in the black-out when he took his express on the relief line.

An overtaking newspaper train just managed to pull clear as the crash happened, avoiding by less than a second the scattering coaches from the express. But twenty seven passengers had been killed in the disaster (in fact, under three percent of the total complement), and Driver Stacey, who sadly admitted his error, died shortly afterwards from, they say, utter dejection during which he lost the will to live, although he had not been injured during the rolling over of his locomotive which killed his fireman.

It was 49 years, 11 months, and 24 days after the previous fatal accident on the Great Western, at the same Somerset junction two miles beyond Taunton.

# 20

# Curious Ticket Request at Queen Street

A booking clerk on duty in the smoky dungeon of Queen Street Low Level on the London and North Eastern Railway, back in 1938, shares the credit for this story of a lady from the remote West Highlands. It went the rounds of Glasgow via that splendid newspaper *The Bulletin* which left us in 1960. It was also credited to a tram conductor by the *Bulletin's* evening partner.

Never having travelled to the big city before, and indeed quite new to railway journeys, the lady from a farm on the Ardnamurchan Peninsula was called urgently by a doctor to see a sick relative in the hospital at Springburn. Her husband after the difficult road trip to Fort William got her a return ticket to Queen Street. Confused, worried, yet fascinated by her first ride on a steam train, she duly arrived at the LNERs terminal in Glasgow. A porter told her that to get to Springburn she must go downstairs to the Low Level and buy a ticket.

This was a complication but she found herself near a ticket window clutching some money. In front of her was a young woman, and she decided to watch the process of obtaining a travel document (for the ten mile ride) from a clerk.

She clutched her piece of pasteboard which had

allowed her to take the train form Fort William to Queen Street and would, apparently, permit her to go back. She listened intently to the young woman, who announced to the clerk:- 'Maryhill, single.' A ticket emerged without, apparently, any further conversation. Now it was her turn. 'Morag McLeod, married,' she volunteered.

---

APPLEDORE in Kent was a junction long ago, when a line branched off the Ashford-Hastings route to serve Lydd and New Romney. In the summer of 1955, I was traveling with a colleague to Lydd, where we were being met and taken to Ferryfield, in those days a successful airport owned by Silver City Airways operating Bristol Freighter car-carrying flights to Le Touquet (at the height of its boom, over 200 services a day were flown on Saturdays).

Our train from Ashford consisted of four ex-Southern Railway Maunsell coaches hauled by an L class 4-4-0, No 31769. At Appledore, the last two coaches were uncoupled to await a 'Mickey Mouse' 2-6-2 tank which was to come in to the platform to take them on to Hastings. But it came too soon, on the wrong line, and with brakes hard on, locked buffers with our L. There was no great harm done, but the half hour delay missed us a flight.

# 21

# Slip Up

THE slip coach was a Great Western Railway innovation, at its height in the period from 1870 to 1939, but used by other railways to a considerable extent. The GWR had more than thirty daily 'slips' in its pre-war timetables, three of them off the *Cornish Riviera Express* to serve Westbury, Taunton and Exeter in order to achieve a non-stop run with the main part of the train to Plymouth.

It is a system which has not been used since 1960, mainly because of the cost. A 'slip-guard' had to be in charge of each section being slipped, and a locomotive had to be on stand-by at the station being served. The last slip was at Bicester.

Slip coaches were used by the London, Brighton, and South Coast Railway, particularly at Polegate to serve Eastbourne. They were even provided as a service to commuters (only that term was not employed in those days), with the Great Eastern Railway slipping coaches at Broxbourne off its Cambridge expresses so that passengers could enjoy a fast service to that town, only seventeen miles from London, and also to Hertford East.

The word 'enjoy' is perhaps not appropriate, since many passengers viewed them with alarm, not wishing to be in part of a train which has broken away, even under control. On the Great Western, some passengers preferred to eschew the fast service to places such as

74

Reading and Westbury and took stopping trains instead. So much depended upon the experience of the guard and his liaison with the driver.

On the dark wet evening of March 7, 1927 the 6.35pm Paddington to Cheltenham, first stop Swindon (like its opposite number in the up-direction, the *Cheltenham Flyer*) was due to slip two coaches for Reading. Misjudging the speed and his position in the murky darkness, the guard slipped prematurely and they came to rest in the blackness of Sonning Cutting.

Slip coaches carried distinctive lights, a red above a white on the rear coach if two were being slipped, a red in line with a white if only one was to come off the train. In the two mile long canyon of Sonning, no one saw these and the signalman at Reading saw the main express go thundering through, correctly assuming the slip portion would come in gently on its own, for which the points were then set to allow it to reach a platform.

But it never came. It sat on the tracks 1½ miles away.

Passengers in the slip coaches were alarmed, some actually terrified. They all knew the procedure and realised something had gone wrong. They feared that the two helpless coaches sitting on the main line would be crashed into by a following express. Trains were passing, although on the inner, slow line to Reading.

The slip-guard, aware of his mistake, had in fact protected his segmented train with detonators and made sure its slip lights were burning brightly. The signalman at Reading realised the slip had failed and acted accordingly. A stand-by tank engine was sent away on 'wrong line working order' (this takes a while to arrange) and it was forty minutes before it reached the stranded coaches. The passengers got to Reading almost an hour late.

Anxieties and protests were such that the 6.35pm express to Cheltenham stopped in its entirety at Reading from that time onwards. But apart from a mention in a local paper and a paragraph in *The Times*, no adverse publicity resulted. The remaining slips (some thirty in all) were maintained throughout the life of the Great Western. Reading, though, was served only in the up direction.

From the very first experimental slip in 1840 on the London and Blackwall Railway, when a guard undid a chain coupling to achieve the effect, until 9 September 1960 when a Western Region express from Paddington to Birmingham slipped for the last time at Bicester, no lives were lost on slip coach operations.

## 22

# The Locomotive That Disappeared into a Black Hole

IN the more prosperous days of the Furness Railway there were active iron ore mines served by its branches. One such mine was reached from Lindal, a station on the main line between Ulverston and Barrow. On a late October day in 1892, soon after eight o'clock on a gloomy morning, an 0-6-0 shunting engine was drifting along the branch siding to Lindal mines to pick up some wagons.

Painted, as were all Furness locomotives, in 'iron-ore red', No 115 was eleven years old, having been built by Sharp Stewart and Company in 1881. Driver Postlethwaite was almost stationary as he saw the wagons ahead of him, but suddenly they seemed to be rising above his engine. The time was 8.16am as the wagons rose higher and higher, or at least they had appeared to do so. He realised that it was their engine which was going down, rather fast, and he yelled to Fireman Robinson to jump out. The driver followed very rapidly, emerging level with his locomotive's steam dome.

The ground had given way and the track plus locomotive sank steadily. Six hours afterwards there was no trace but a black hole, and by next day sounding reported the engine to be some 200ft below the surface! It was never recovered and the hole was filled in with waste ore and ballast.

---

IN the summer of 1962 the 5.30pm Oxford to Paddington nonstop was the fastest steam train in the world, averaging 63.5mph. But there was only a decimal point of difference between this train and an evening express out of Paris Est to Belfort hauled by a former Chemin de Fer de L'Est *Mountain* over the Troyes to Chaumont section. Both vied with each other that summer and clipped minutes off their runs.

Riding the footplate of No 7030 *Cranbrook Castle* one evening in June from Oxford, when we completed the run to London in 54 minutes, 20 seconds despite a signal check at Didcot, I was told by Fireman Alan Trego that he corresponded regularly with the fireman on the French train (who was regularly assigned to the job). 'He writes to me in English, sending his logs, and I write back in French, sending ours. This run is our best yet.'

But the Indian summer did not last long. By the next year, Western Region had replaced its express with a semi-fast diesel train taking twenty-seven minutes longer, and diesels took over on the Paris-Basle line. Enthusiasm was irrevocably doused.

# 23

---

# 'Close the Windows'

---

WATER troughs, like so many railway ideas, were invented in Britain, Ramsbottom put in the first set on the North Wales line as early as 1859. The United States was the only other country to develop the idea, where they were called 'track pans' (a term that had an entirely different meaning in the United Kingdom; 'track pans' were those long metal troughs which were slid under sleeping cars lying stationary in main line stations before the days of retension toilets).

France did for a while have a couple of sets of water troughs on the Chemin de Fer de L'Ouest line to Bordeaux, when there was a little competition for the important Bordeaux traffic between the wars.

In Britain there were simply dozens of sets, enabling fast non-stop running for which the private railways of Britain were famous. Only the Southern Railway had none, somehow achieving its longest and fastest non-stop run with the pre-war *Bournemouth Limited* with a Schools class 4-4-0 and a very carefully watched water supply in the tender. The run called for the 108 miles to be covered in 115 minutes.

Most regular passengers knew where and when to expect the water troughs and had the windows closed well in advance if they were in a coach near the engine. They did the same thing with tunnels. People in corner seats who took no precautions could get quite wet if the fireman's scoop hit the water above 65mph.

There were no less than nine sets of troughs between London Euston and Carlisle, laid not only with the intention of replenishing the tender but to store the best and softest water which could be found. Hard and chalky water did eventual damage to boilers, which was probably the main reason why the Southern and its earlier constituents never laid them.

One of those nine troughs on the former LMSR caused problems for some colleagues on a train I was taking from Heysham to Euston in the autumn of 1961. We were a small, privileged group riding in a special dining car attached directly behind the Class 5 locomotive. This engine, with nine 'on' attained a fair turn of speed once up the short steep hill from Lancaster, and was running at nearly 80 mph by Garstang. Knowing that Brock Troughs were coming very shortly, I closed the fanlight above my elegantly laid table. Abundant drinks had already been served and there was a special meal about to be presented.

It was an unusually warm, early October day, and my four colleagues across the way had their fanlight window full open. I lifted my glass upwards, trying to indicate the window and said, 'Troughs, gentlemen.' They raised theirs and replied 'Troughs to you.' They should have known better, or at least two of them should. One was John Carter, the eminent presenter of television's *Wish You Were Here*, then a journalist on newspapers. His father was a noted Great Western railway offical and John knew his way about trains. Opposite him sat the late Colonel Geoffrey Portham, who came from a railway engineering family.

The scoop hit at eighty and the rush of water over the diner was intense. It drenched the four of them, Geoffrey Portham (facing the engine) in particular. The table, soaked and dripping, looked as if half of Brock Troughs had emptied on to it in a few seconds.

Having their luggage with them enabled two of the half drowned victims to retire for a complete change of clothes. The chief steward was angry as he mopped up and relayed the table. 'Oh, gentlemen, gentlemen, why didn't you close the window... you were warned.'

But taking water at speed can have more serious consequences. In 1939, two of the famous streamlined trains of the LNER the up and down *Coronations*, were scheduled to pass each other near Darlington. They were the only streamliners to pass, for the *Silver Jubilee* and *West Riding Limited* were composed of stock which made the round trip. Just north of Northallerton lay the Wiske Moor Water Troughs, and due to the late running of the northbound train (delayed by about ten minutes south of Peterborough) the streamliners met on the troughs at a combined speed of 170mph.

The maelstrom of water between the two trains hurled coal off the northbound engine's tender and windows were smashed in the first coach, not only drenching but injuring several passengers. The southbound express was undamaged but the northbound had to make a stop at Darlington to sort out the damage and minor casualties. With an evacuated first coach, the *Coronation* recorded one of its rare late arrivals in Edinburgh, more than an hour behind time. Special precautions were taken to ensure that they never met on water troughs again for the mere three months left to them, before World War II eliminated the high speed trains and their magnificent standards for ever.

# 24

# Misunderstanding at Paddington

THE elderly gentleman arriving off a train from Henley-on-Thames was a typical Englishman, unwilling to accept change and 'foreign notions'. The railway system had just introduced the twenty-four hour clock, but that meant little or nothing to this passenger.

Intent upon an early dinner with a friend in town and a theatre visit, he enquired from a ticket inspector the time of the last train back to Henley. 'Twenty-two eleven,' he was told.

The passenger arrived back at Paddington at half past ten with, he supposed, just over ten minutes to catch his train. To his intense chagrin, he discovered that it had already gone. His protests got him up the stairs of platform 1 to the area manager's office, where it was explained to him that his train had left on time at 22.11, and that the interpretation he had put upon it, 22,40 (or twenty to eleven in old parlance) was wrong.

However, Western Region were kind on this occasion, and arranged to have him met at Twyford off the last Reading local with a free taxi to take him home to Henley.

# 25

# Ghost Horse
# at Glenfinnan

Amoung the many stories and legends that are told about the heroic building of the West Highland Railway, and the extension to Mallaig, is the one about the horse and cart reputed to have fallen into the concrete of a pillar. In his 1965 book *The West Highland Railway*, John Thomas devoted a paragraph to the story he suggested 'may be apocryphal' about a horse being led with a cart over planking resting temporarily across the top of a column which was being filled with liquid concrete.

The horse is said to have slipped and to have gone over the planking followed by the cart while the man leading the animal jumped clear. It was 100ft down to the still liquid concrete and both horse and cart disappeared from view. It was impossible to retrieve them so the order was given to continue filling the pillar with the vast amounts of concrete used on the building.

Robert McAlpine of Glasgow was the contractor for the West Highland and later the Mallaig extension. His use of concrete earned him the nickname - much used by cruise train commentators to this day - 'Concrete Bob'. For five years the Mallaig Railway was the greatest concentration of concrete construction in the world. Its great works stand today, virtually untouched , as a memorial to him.

But weather conditions can be savage in the extreme along both lines, especially over Rannoch Moor and along the exposed stretch at Glenfinnan where the sea winds drive in from the Atlantic up the Glen past the Bonnie Prince Charlie monument (which marks his departure from the scene as much as the raising of his Standard in 1745) at the head of Loch Shiel. In fact, for Bonnie Prince Charlie this was his first and last appearance on the Scottish Mainland; he was to wander through the islands, to Uist and to Skye, aided by Flora MacDonald, until his final rescue by a French ship.

Until the coming of the railway at the turn of the century and the building of the Glenfinnan Viaduct this was as remote and inaccessible a spot as could be imagined. The wild sealochs of the North West, remote though they were and still are, had access by sea, and fishermen knew them. Not so Glenfinnan, nor even Glencoe.

But there are times when the wet winds ease, and fine, clear and even very warm weather takes over. It happened in the late spring of 1989, when Fort William and Lochaber had the highest temperatures in the British Isles. It had also happened in 1976 and 1984.

Engineers' inspection teams check the great viaduct, and others less dramatic, along the West Highland line, going across it in a suitably equipped vehicle and viewing the underside from lowered wooden platforms with rope ladders attached.

But in recent years, cruise trains have stopped at Glenfinnan long enough for groups of passengers to walk to the monument. The regular steam train service, the *Lochaber*, made the Glenfinnan stop for a while and let passengers off, although it now runs fast to complete the Fort William-Mallaig trip in 100 minutes with only one stop for passing a Super-Sprinter.

It did mean that groups of people were afoot in the

region of the viaduct, and some inspected its great pillars from below. In May of 1989, a number of men and one or two ladies, lightly dressed in the unaccustomed brilliant sunshine and heat, wandered among its twenty-one concrete spans. Towards the base of the fifth column, where the concrete was worn thin, they saw it.

Two or three of them photographed what was quite clearly the outline of an axled vehicle and nearby the rib cage of a large animal. None knew of the legend of the horse and cart from construction days. But they told people on the train and word got about among the West Highlands.

The next time a group of 'Sassenachs' walked up from the Bonnie Prince Charlie monument, and it was not more than a week later, they saw that fresh concrete and paint had been liberally plastered on the fifth column. There was nothing unusual showing through. As for those who had taken photographs, one had a few blanks, while the others showed close-ups of a pillar of Glenfinnan Viaduct, with no outline on it.

# 26

# Leaves on the Lines

IN recent years a cause for delay on the Southern Region of British Railways has been autumnal leaves on the lines. Many third-rail electric trains have been affected by this, to the chagrin of commuters, especially the older ones who never experienced this problem, even during gale-swept autumns with heavy leaf fall.

The two reasons are, of course, cut down and cut-back. There used to be sufficient track maintenance men employed to see that there was never an unreasonable build-up of leaves, while others cut back the overlapping trees. Various 'hi-tec' methods are now being developed to reduce or eliminate the problem.

However, on 15 November 1983 the leaves claimed a prestigious victim - the British day-Pullmans of the Venice Simplon *Orient Express* on its return journey from Folkestone to Victoria with a full load aboard, including passengers from Venice, and day trip passengers who had gone down by motor coach via Leeds Castle to join the luxury train at Folkestone.

The diesel hauling the rake of nine heavy Pullmans plus the converted former LNER baggage van cleared Maidstone on the secondary line successfully but gradually lost speed, coming to a halt shortly after passing West Malling station. A great deal of snarling and shuddering came from the struggling diesel but the train did not move. Torches flashing in the rain and darkness outside the train quickly led to confirmation that an abundance of leaves had caused the stall.

This being the new 'modern' railway, there was no telephone in the cab, nor were there any signal boxes with phoning points nearby. Help, the guard decided, must come from a station, and he bade a temporary farewell to the passengers as he set out to walk back to West Malling along the track. Champagne and other drinks were brought out to apease the stranded passengers. But after an hour, the guard had not returned, and nothing had happened apart from the passing of electric trains eastbound.

When, eventually, after nearly two hours, a drenched and mud-bespattered guard did climb back on the train he was regaled with hot coffee and what was left of the scones and jam aboard the train, while passengers gathered round to hear his story.

Making sure his train was fully protected at the rear, he had walked along the track gingerly keeping away from the live third rail where wet leaves might have caused a shock or worse, lighting his way with a torch and his lamp.

He reached West Malling station platform after about ten minutes. But after climbing the ramp he found it was closed and completely unattended. There was, however, a phone box, but on trying to use it, he found it was totally out of action.

Regaining the tracks he plodded on through the rain, soon coming across a stranded electric train, whose driver sought news of what was happening. The signal showed red, of course, set by a distant signal control centre. Both guard and driver would have wished to make direct contact with that centre.

The VSOE Pullman guard continued his walk, and after just over a mile he saw the lights of a second stranded electric, full of fuming passengers, many it seemed, with West End theatre tickets wasting away in their wallets and handbags. He gave the news to the irate driver and plodded along for another quarter of a mile on to the ramp of East Malling station. Here he was indeed 'lucky' for a single member of the station staff was still on duty. Contact was made fairly quickly with Swanley where a spare diesel locomotive was more or less available. This, he was told, would set out shortly on wrong line working and come to the rescue. But it had to make a journey of seventeen miles to the stalled Pullman train and this might take half an hour.

The VSOE guard was told that a bus would pass by the station fairly soon and he was advised to take it to the road 'near his train'. It arrived within ten minutes, and he boarded it, though required to pay a 40p fare. He wiped his window frequently, hoping to see the lights of the Pullman, but when he did spot them they seemed a long way away across fields. Persuading the bus driver to let him out at an unauthorised stop, he climbed a fence and aimed in what he thought was the right direction to his train. Twice he fell in ditches and at the final fence, clambering over to reach the tracks, he tore his trousers. It had not stopped raining during the whole of his solitary expedition of rescue.

Eventually, the relief diesel did arrive and together with the train engine and some shovelling, the VSOE Pullmans were dragged clear of their soggy obstruction. In about half an hour, the Swanley engine detached leaving the train engine to continue to Victoria, which it did successfully in forty minutes, being very much out of course. The train arrived three hours late, and the backed-up electrics recorded lateness of two and one hour respectively.

Some 800 passengers were badly delayed, more than 100 theatre seats were unfilled, and about 200 dinner table reservations were lost. As one of the passengers on the VSOE that day, I hope the guard was refunded his 40p and given a new pair of trousers.

# 27

# 'I am the President of France'

IT was the autumn of 1926, before the days of talking pictures, when theatrical touring companies from England, speaking English, were especially popular in many part of Europe. One such small company, of eight players and a director, was gathered at Victoria station to join the 2pm boat train to Dover Marine.

They boarded the heavy, comfortable wooden-panelled stock of the Southern Railway Company's second class, occupying two compartments, enjoying tea served by a waiter on the pull-out table which was to be found in such rolling stock at the time, and indeed for the next ten years. This was really a through ticket convenience, with most Britons travelling abroad in those days riding 2:1:2 or 3:1:2, meaning second or third on the English train, first class on the steamer (they were not called ferries then) and second class on the Continent.

The actors were bound for Calais to join the through sleeping cars of the *Orient Express*, which would be hauled, with a dining car attached, south-south-east across France to join the main train at Chalons. The main part of the *Orient Express* left Paris East at five minutes to eight in the evening to reach Chalons at 9.46pm. The English who travelled by such trains never bothered with the Continent's twenty-four hour clock.

Contrary to modern beliefs, fostered by the operators of restored vintage trains, the Venice Simplon *Orient Express* and the 'Nostalgie Instanbul Orient Express' in particular, the 'Trains de Luxe' carried second class passengers. In fact, they were composed of first and second class sleepers, a diner, and baggage fourgons (one or two of the latter equipped with relatively primitive showers). There were no piano bars, nor observation saloons and Pullmans.

When our actors reached Calais they transferred to the blue and gold Wagons-Lits waiting in the Maritime station, and took up their two berth compartments, which were at each end of the sleeper. The single berth first class sleepers were towards the centre, where the riding qualities were kinder.

It was not long before they heard the rumour, soon to be confirmed, that a travelling companion on the *Orient Express* would be the President of France. Security was minimal in Europe of the 1920s, and not until King Alexander of Yugo-Slavia was assassinated in Marseilles in 1935 was it tightened up in France.

The main part of the train was sitting at Chalons station, one of the new 'Mountain' class 4-8-2 locomotives of the Chemin de Fer de L'Est simmering at his head, when the Calais coaches arrived. The Calais restaurant was detached, and their two sleepers were fitted into the heavy train. The President, passengers heard, was in the next Wagon-Lit, occupying a first class compartment and with his valet and secretary sharing a second at the end of the car.

The *Orient Express* left a few minutes after ten o'clock, and ran non-stop to Strasbourg. After that it wended its way across Germany, through Kehl and Karlsruhe, Stuttgart and Ulm, towards Munich where it was due at 8.24am. Sometime around seven o'clock, the President's valet brought a pot of coffee to his master's door. He had obtained it from the attendant, who, it seems did not have the privilege of serving the President of France. But he did have the privilege, after repeated knocks on the door, of producing a key and some manipulative instruments in case the bolts were shot. They were not needed; the door opened easily enough.

But the President was not there. His bed had been slept in, but his nightgown or nightshirt (which he always wore) was missing.

Panic ensued. The train was brought to a halt well short of Augsburg. The British theatrical company was awakened. But no one knew anything and no one had seen him. The *Orient Express* was allowed to proceed to Augsburg where the police were alerted urgently and the French consul awakened.

Someone noticed that the end door of the Wagon-Lit was not properly closed. This, then, was how he had been abducted. But where? And by whom?

Soon all was resolved. The President was safe, but he was back in France. A car was being sent for him and he would make his way to his official engagements in Austria later. The *Orient Express* was allowed to proceed.

It was several months before the English actors heard the real story of what had happened to the President of France.

It happened in 1926, the era of the Third Republic, and Gaston Doumergue - then aged sixty three - occupied the presidency. He quite literally fell out of the *Orient Express*. However, he lived until 1937 and was more fortunate than his successor, Paul Doumer, who was assassinated in 1931 after less than a full year in office. This began the need, expanded in this day and age, of bodyguards, but Monsieur Doumergue had only two staff with him, neither armed and one of them academic.

Somewhere about one o'clock in the morning, the President - who had wined and dined well in his compartment and consumed a full bottle of chilled

Champagne - awoke and felt an urgent call of nature. He got out of bed in his nightshirt, found a pair of slippers, and made his way along the lurching corridor to the end of the Wagon-Lit, bemoaning, no doubt, the absence of private facilities and not apparently aware of the small china pot provided in the compactum of these new (1924) sleeping cars.

He opened the wrong door, the trains' 'slipstream' swinging it wide and lifting the metal steps which gave him a boost - out wards. He was lucky in two respects. The train was climbing gently and running at only 35mph. And the boost sent him onto the grassy embarkment, down which he rolled, coming to rest more or less unhurt as the tail-light of his train disappeared round a curve.

Somehow the elderly gentleman managed to struggle up the slope to the tracks and tottered in the direction of the train, perhaps hoping his fall had been observed and that it had stopped for him. Eventually, he saw the lights of a tall signal 'Poste', and, reaching it, staggered up the steps and hammered on the door.

The lone signalman saw through the glass a rather old man, his greying hair unkempt, clad in a dirty nightshirt and wearing battered slippers. It was to his credit that he opened the door, although taking the precaution of arming himself with an iron poker from the fireplace.

A plaintive voice came to him out of the darkness. 'Let me in. I am the President of France.'

Inevitably, the signalman replied, 'Yes, and I am the Emperor Napoleon.'

It took more than an hour before the unfortunate President convinced the signalman that he was, indeed, the President and had fallen out of the *Orient Express* and not an escapee from the local mad house.

By this time the train had entered Germany and it took a good deal of action with phones to the police and across the border to German rail officials before the express was stopped between Ulm and Augsburg.

# 28

# The Big Sneeze

DRIVER Jack Sharp of King's Cross top shed was prone to explosive sneezes, especially when exposed to a combination of dust and brilliant sunlight. One very sunny and warm day in August 1960, when leaning out of the cab of his Gresley V2 2-6-2 locomotive hauling an up *Cambridge Buffet Express*, it not only brought the train to a standstill for about half an hour but led to a managerial enquiry.

The Cambridge Buffet Car expresses were long established favourites on the fifty-eight mile run from the University City to London. In pre-war days they had been known as the Garden Cities Expresses stopping only at Letchworth Garden City and Welwyn Garden City on the way to King's Cross. Hauled invariably by an Ivatt Atlantic, they consisted of six coaches, one of which was a Gresley buffet car which remained open until the very platform end at the terminus and served meals at seats with a speed and accuracy never equalled on the rails. The time allowed was eighty-two minutes.

After the war, they were slow to restart, and when they did more coaches were added and the motive power was usually a V2. Places along the line had grown in importance and stops were added so that the timing extended out to ninety minutes. Royston, Hitchin, and Stevenage were called at in addition to the two Garden Cities, but the 3.15pm from Cambridge managed the journey in eighty-five minutes, omitting the Royston stop. This was the most popular train among university people coming to London for dinners, the theatre and various other purposes.

It was the 3.15pm that Driver Jack Sharp was taking to London when he sneezed. It was just outside Brookmans Park, about three miles on the London side of Hatfield. His teeth shot out of his mouth as his nasal passages exploded even more violently than usual, triggered by coal dust and the sunshine as he leaned out of the cab at 65mph.

Immediately he applied the brakes for an emergency stop.'I'm not going to lose those false teeth,' he spluttered to his fireman as he dropped down on the track. He found them half a mile back, well clear of the train, undamaged on the lineside grasses. Returning to his engine at a jog-trot, waving to faces hanging out of lowered windows and shouting to an irate guard, he got his train started but lost his path to suburban workings and arrived half an hour late. The subsequent enquiry put a disciplinary mark against his name and he went on freight duties, retiring soon after with what he alleged to be a pension of only 1s/11½d (10p) a week!

# 29

# Galloway Bulls

THE directors of the London, Midland and Scottish Railway were very keen on building hotels in the early 1930s. The success of Gleneagles, started as a great luxury concept by the Caledonian Railway in 1914 but finished by the LMS in 1924, led them towards planning modern resort complexes.

At Morecambe they erected the Midland, the only one on the beach side of the promenade, reached by their own tracks. This hotel, with some aspects of its architecture taken from an ocean liner, is still a showpiece, although it ceased to be a railway hotel back in 1950.

The biggest venture of all was planned for the south west of Scotland, where no top hotels existed. It was to be a 'Gleneagles of Galloway', complete with golf courses, and it would be linked to Gatehouse of Fleet railway station, on the Dumfries to Stranraer line (destroyed under the Beeching Act in 1965). Gatehouse of Fleet station must be the worst located of any station in Britain in relation to its village, some eight miles away. But it would be ideal for the luxury sporting complex.

Wall Street had not yet crashed so prosperity continued to reign on both sides of the Atlantic that spring of 1929. However, the people of that part of Galloway, mostly sturdy farmers with little imagination, were greatly opposed to their land and their peace being invaded by the whim of a railway company.

One day a special train arrived with directors and invited guests. They made their way over the fields to the heart of the projected site. Suddenly there were some roars and several giant black Galloway bulls (the fiercest in Britain, noted for their belt of white hide) charged the assembled gathering. Somehow the VIPs escaped alive, although two were injured.

The train left hurriedly and the directors cancelled the Galloway project. That money was allocated to the Queens Hotel, Leeds, to make it the best equipped in the north. It had, and still has, private bathrooms in all its rooms, but someone forgot the lavatories.

# 30

# Connel Ferry Conflict

AN interesting branch line in the Highlands used to
take passengers on a twenty-eight mile ride through
glorious country to the edge of historic Glencoe. It was
the Connel Ferry to Ballachulish line, carrying three
trains every weekday, a fourth on Saturdays, and nothing
on Sundays.

However, there was a snag and that snag was the
Connel Ferry Bridge across the sea inlet Loch Etive at its
narrowest part. This was shared by road traffic. In the
days of rail dominance, trains had complete priority; in
later years this weakened, and under the Beeching holocaust, with the road lobby ever stronger, the line was
closed.

There used to be a single line working for road traffic,
but the road was so close to the railway line that in the
interests of safety all road traffic had to be stopped before
a train could be accepted. A railwayman inhabited a hut
at the North Connel end of the half mile of bridge. He
controlled road traffic at his end by hand and at the other
end by a traffic indicator.

When a train was due he would stop traffic both ways
and close a gate against the road at his end. This released
a key with which he locked the traffic indicator lever,
which he could only do if the indicator was at stop. This
released another key. The man then climbed on his

bicycle and rode over to the Connel Ferry end where he would unlock the gate across the railway, swinging it over across the road. This action released another key with which he could unlock the signal frame and pull-off for the train. When this had cleared the bridge he had to do all this in reverse.

The process prevented road traffic for about twelve minutes, six times a day (eight times on Saturdays). A few tempers may have frayed in rare hot weather in pre-war days but generally the system was accepted with calm Highland courtesy. Only after the lifting of petrol rationing and the encouragement of car ownership at all levels from 1951 onwards were there outbursts of wrath and bad behaviour by road users. Even fire engines had to wait, and the Oban brigade was called out on occasions to blazes in Appin.

One day in the late 1950s an ambulance on a vitally urgent mission felt it could not wait - and did not. It charged the gate and crossed against an oncoming train. The driver of the *Caledonian* 0-4-4 tank hauling two coaches and two wagons at 15mph came to a stop. The ambulance squeezed by, grinding against the coaches with a mutual loss of paint. The horrified bridgeman rode his bike wildly across the bridge, used his key, and saved the north end gate by seconds.

# 31

## Dreaming of a Driver's Cap

Miss Beatrice Newman, who lived in the west country, used to dream periodically and her dreams seemed very real. She had recounted a few of them to her friends and relatives and some came true in varying degrees.

One night Miss Newman dreamed of Cornish holidays, when something came sharply into focus. It was an engine driver's cap with the unmistakeable oil cloth protecting its top. In her dream she picked it up, sure that it represented some kind of railway accident. But there was no wreckage in her dream, nor were bodies scattered around. The cap bore no name, just Great Western Railway, Penzance.

Next day, with most of the dream clear in her mind, she told one or two friends, and scanned the newspapers as well as listening to the radio. But nothing had happened on the railway to make news.

Three days later, her weekly newspaper dropped through the letter box. And there was an item which made her heart leap. She rushed round to the friends to whom she had told the story of her latest dream. The item said:- 'Driver's narrow escape on the Great Western! Driver William Travannion, on the footplate of a goods engine travelling through Cornwall, was leaning from his cab when the engine seemed to hit a rough patch of track. He lost his grip and was thrown from the cab to fall on the lineside. His fireman stopped the train within half a mile and alerted the guard. Together they rushed back along the track and met their driver staggering towards them. He had been only slightly injured but had lost his cap. Driver Travannion comes from Penzance'.

# 32

# Aglow with Fire

DRIVER William Thomas of Bristol was taking a diesel unit on a late evening stopping service from Bath to Temple Meads. It was in April, 1956, and the unit he controlled was a former Great Western Railway diesel, No W35, consisting of power car and a trailer, also powered. It was the 9.8pm from Bath due Bristol 9.34

The service was running late due to a malfunctioning engine and shortly before Saltford smoke and flames were found coming from one of the engines. Guard Albert Hulin, a former member of the Wolverhampton Fire Brigade, used an extinguisher on the blaze, while Driver Thomas, who had spent 43 of his 59 years with the railway, took a second extinguisher to make sure the fire was completely out.

At Saltford, possibly because of the alarm, the few remaining passengers got out of the train. There were seven miles to run before reaching Bristol, but the train started up and soon entered the long Fox's Wood Tunnel between Keynsham and St Anne's Park. Looking behind him, Driver Thomas saw a red glow expanding and realised the train was on fire again, this time seriously.

It was a nightmare journey through the tunnel and out into the night. Driver Thomas accelerated as hard as he could, deliberately passing a red signal light under the emergency pressure. Guard Hulin was cut off, unable to get through to the driver's compartment.

Duty Porter Edward Newman at St Anne's station heard the train approaching and looked under the foot-bridge, to see a veritable fireball on its way. The guard had leapt clear, but Driver Thomas hung on to his controls even with the fire bursting into his compart-ment. He stopped just short of the platform and leapt out, injuring his ankle, but stumbled on to the platform where he was joined by the guard and porter. They phoned for the fire brigade but before that arrived the inferno on the track exploded, the ten gallons of diesel in the leading tank went up and set fire to the embankment.

The signalman in the nearest box blocked both tracks. Despite his injury, Driver Thomas, aided by Guard Hulin, went back to the wreck of their train and managed to evacuate all the parcels and mail from the last compartment. These were singed but not destroyed.

Totally ruined, the old Great Western unit remained on the tracks and the burned-out cars were towed to Temple Meads by a pannier tank. So rapid was the clearance of the line (in contrast to these days) that the 10.55pm was able to run from Bath to Bristol.

# 33

## Body on the Line

THE electric-hauled 'Manchester Pullman' was travelling fast through the autumnal dusk of a Friday night in September 1988. A waiter serving four diners faltered for a moment and looked very alarmed.

'What's the matter?' asked a businessman. The waiter, whose features were returning to normal, replied with slight hesitation that everything was all right. But having served the table he hurried away in search of the chief steward.

'I've just seen a body. Out of the window. Lying beside the line, it was. On the left hand side of the train.'

'Where, exactly? Think hard. How long ago.'

'Somewhere around Wilmslow. I'm not sure. I just looked up and straight out of the window and there it was. We passed it in a flash.'

'Well, we stopped at Wilmslow. Was it before or after the station?'

'I can't say for sure. I was very busy all the time, and we were going at some lick.'

'Must have been before Wilmslow. We haven't gone very fast since then, with only half a dozen miles to the stop at Stockport. Look, we're stopping there now. I'll try and tell someone or else report it at Manchester.'

It was too late, with no staff nearby on the station, to do anything about it at Stockport but less than ten minutes later the chief steward reported the sighting. By now it was almost dark, but officials quickly alerted trains and stations to the probable existence of a dead body on the lineside in the Wilmslow area.

All trains slowed as their drivers and guards watched carefully on the down side of the line. Significant delays occurred to all Manchester traffic which even affected the west coast main, as Crewe connections were slowed. Nothing was found.

The Manchester police took the matter very seriously and questioned the waiter in detail.

When working on a train, concentrating upon table orders, and going into the largely windowless kitchen car, it is not easy to be aware of one's exact location. Passengers who sometimes ask dining car staff where the train is are probably more aware of its position than the waiters, especially these days when so many landmarks including smaller stations with nameboards have ceased to exist.

The waiter could not be more explicit, but it was agreed that he must have seen the body something like five miles south of Wilmslow. The police were certain that he had seen a body for his description and sincerity convinced them. It was, he said, in bright clothing.

At first light, a police helicopter was sent up, equipped with a heat-seeking device which is supposed to detect corpses which have been dead for up to a day.

Flown low, once in each direction between Wilmslow and the outskirts of Crewe, the helicopter trip failed to spot anything unusual. Trains were again alerted to the mystery and more delays resulted from slow speeds over some thirty miles of track as drivers and train staff peered into the morning light. They, too found nothing.

A British Rail party set out on foot from Sandbach and searched carefully. Less than a mile from Chelford station they found it: a full size Orville Duck, garishly clad.

# 34

# The Chairman
# Changes at Crewe

WHEN the affable and popular Sir Peter Parker was Chairman of British Railways, he undertook numerous journeys and speaking engagements. He had a good knowledge of railways worldwide, and retained an affection for steam locomotives 'in their place'. It was under his chairmanship that the 'Return to Steam' movement succeeded, and he rode with a special behind *King George V*.

Once, seated next to him at dinner in London, I asked him which steam locomotive, or class of locomotive, had produced the best return on capital expended upon them.

He replied that it was a single tank engine, one supplied to China in the early days, which not only earned much revenue from working a thirty mile route but was later sold for three times what it had cost!

His knowledge, however, came unstuck one day in the early 1970s when, with an aide, he was travelling to Blackpool to speak at a dinner-meeting, and broke his journey for some business in Crewe. With Sir Peter leading and in a hurry, the two men re-entered the famous junction station and leapt aboard a first class coach in a rake of rolling stock changing engines, as trains did in those days from electric to diesel and vice-versa.

It was the wrong train. It was an express to London, proudly scheduled to do the 158 miles in one hour, fifty-nine minutes! Alarmed but not willing to pull a communication cord for his own mistake, Sir Peter went along the corridor to talk with the guard. This individual was a keen Union man and took rather a delight in the discomfiture of the chairman.

'No Sir, I can only stop the train in an emergency, and this is not a real one. It's your mistake.'

Recognising that he could scarcely force the issue in the circumstances, Sir Peter entered a lavatory and collected a roll of toilet paper. He wrote messages on it, requesting station staff to telephone Blackpool to tell them what had happened. 'I am Sir Peter Parker, Chairman of BR, on the wrong train. Please phone Blackpool 2… and tell them I cannot attend.

He hurled this fairly heavy roll out of the window as the train ran through Stafford at a relatively sedate 55mph. He saw it bounce along a platform and unfurl. In case of message damage, he repeated the process from a second lavatory and threw this roll out at Rugeley. This hit a station building and looked to be intact.

With his aide, the Chairman did some work in the compartment until Euston was reached on time. They were slow to alight, discussing whether to phone a full explanation to Blackpool from the Chairman's Office, then at Rail House.

As they stepped down from the first class coach two burly Transport Police came up to them. 'Now then, you two, we have reports that you were throwing toilet rolls out of the train. Is that true? You don't look like hooligans - just drunk I suppose.'

'Well, yes, we did but…'

'In that case you will please come along with us.'

'But I am Sir Peter Parker, Chairman of British

Railways...'
'Oh yes, and I am the Commissioner of Police.'
It took several minutes before the embarrassed Chairman and equally embarrassed railway officials called to the scene sorted out the problem. The messages thrown out did not get through, and urgent phoning to Blackpool was required.

---

A COUPLE, bound for Earlswood in Surrey one afternoon in the summer of 1991, changed at Redhill and boarded a stopping train. Unlike Salfords, further down the line. Earlswood claims to be open all day and not just at peak hours. However, the announcer did not include it on the list of stops to Brighton, so a check was made by the husband, who was told the train would, indeed, stop at Earlswood. Just before departure, the announcer added the station to the list of stops.

The electric accelerated away and gathered speed, making no effort to stop. It tore through Salfords as well, and came to rest at Horley, five miles from Redhill and four beyond Earlswood. Rushing up to the cab, the couple saw a driver and a girl assistant seated there. On being reminded of their failure to stop, the girl looked through a working timetable. 'We should have stopped at Earlswood,' she told the driver. That worthy did not seem worried. 'Sorry, mate, but there'll be a train on the other platform going back there soon.' With that he started his train.

# 35

# Phantom of Primrose Hill

I heard it as recently as early September, 1990. Others have heard it over the years. Railwaymen sometimes hear it and put on a sickly grin. It may not be heard for a year or more. I first heard it in 1955, but I must have travelled through Primrose Hill Tunnel hundreds of times since then, only hearing it for the second time some thirty-five years later.

We hear, of course, the famous Gresley chime whistle, clear and unmistakable, mostly when a train is stopped at signals on the way in to Euston, but occasionally from a train in motion going north. Friends of mine on the railways have heard it up to half a dozen times when heading for the London Midland main line, once well into Primrose Hill Tunnel.

Gresley locomotives have been through the tunnel, during the locomotive exchanges of 1923 and 1948. Their distinctive chimes really belong to the streamliners, so one would accept that the legend belongs to the latter exchanges. An original A3 such as *Flying Scotsman* would never have sounded it in 1923.

How, then, do we explain the strange event of a late autumn day in 1936 when the 10.40am from Euston to Liverpool, hauled by a 'Jubilee', heard the eerie chime whistle? Fireman Charlie Higgins of Liverpool, was shovelling hard when the Gresley notes sounded. He dropped the coal all over the floor of the cab and at that moment a tongue of flame leapt from the firebox, fired the loose coal, and severely burned him and his cab-mate, Driver John Ball.

In great pain, the driver managed to get his train to Willesden Junction, where assistance was on hand quickly and the two men were taken to Central Middlesex Hospital. After a couple of bad nights they became fairly comfortable and told their story, pointing out that they had expected an engine to be heading at them on the same track, so loud was the whistle, and 'Strange it was, just like those new locos they've got at King's Cross.'

# 36

## Tail Light in the Air

THE driver knew as soon as they had booked on at Camden Shed and started to run the Royal Scot class locomotive down to an evening express to Manchester standing in Euston Station. A kind hearted veteran, the driver did not want to 'shop' his mate for a rare over-indulgence at the pub. He reckoned that if some really hard shovelling was done up the bank the fireman would sweat and sober up fairly quickly.

Swaying on the footplate and somewhat incoherent, the fireman got to work with his shovel and missed being seen by an inspector. Following the right-away, the Royal Scot made a very impressive climb with her heavy train, roaring into the gathering darkness and leaving her banker behind. The driver, seeing his mate firing like a man possessed, thought that all would soon be well as speed increased rapidly through Willesden Junction.

But suddenly the exhausted fireman, still in a hazy state, straightened up and fell against the vacuum brake. This brought the express to an abrupt and unwelcome slowing, corrected only at the last minute by the driver, when the engine was able to accelerate away through Hendon.

Knowing that the guard, a strict and conscientious man, would have logged the emergency slowing when he could see from his windows that the signals were clearly green, the driver decided to continue covering for his inebriated fireman. During the Rugby stop, he wrote his own report, hopefully to coincide with that of the guard. It remains a classic in the LMS archives, even though it was many years before the true cause was revealed.

'I passed the Hendon distant at a good speed as it was "off" but was horrified to see ahead a red light showing the outer home at danger. I made an immediate brake application too late to realise that the red was the tail light of a low flying aeroplane.'

# 37

# Just Short of the Bridge

SCOTLAND'S biggest outdoor party was staged over a period of seven hours on Sunday, 7 October 1990 at and around the Forth Bridge. After a Saturday of violent gales and the largest amount of rain ever to fall in the Edinburgh area (4.19in), the red ochre mass of the great bridge across the Forth shimmered clean and fresh in the brilliant sunshine on the day of the party.

An afternoon of aerial acrobatics, yachting manoeuvres, jugglers and pipers on shore, entertained the increasing crowds until darkness when upwards of 200,000 people crammed into every available vantage point of both shores waited for the spectacle to come

I was among a privileged group which embarked on the Inchcolm ferry *Maid of the Forth* for a view from the middle of the estuary between the road suspension bridge and the magnificent railway bridge. We joined the elegant P&O ship *St Clair* which had on board HRH Prince Edward and many dignitaries including Sir Bob Reid, a man of Fife and the chairman (appointed earlier in 1990) of British Rail. These two vessels were the only ones allowed afloat on the Forth between the hours of 6.30pm and 9.30pm.

A firework display of such colossal brilliance and noise that it had only once been exceeded in Britain (at the Silver Jubilee of Queen Elizabeth II in Hyde Park in 1977) was supported by the swinging beams of thirty-five searchlights. Synchronised with the visual display was a commentary relayed to all watchers, ending with the switching on of the bridge floodlights which will stay on every night until the year 2000. The climax was the reopening of the bridge (closed since 7am) by the handsome A4 Pacific *Osprey* (which has now resumed its original name, *Union of South Africa*) hauling 14 coaches across.

The first part of the commentary told the tragic story of the first bridge across the Tay and Sir Thomas Bouch's start on a Forth bridge, with light illuminating the surviving pillar of his design. A moment's silence was asked in memory of the seventy-five souls who had perished in the waters of the Tay in December 1879 when the Dundee-bound train from the north shore of the Forth had gone down with Bouch's bridge in gale conditions not significantly worse than the ferocity and drenching experienced by most watchers the day before our centenary celebrations. The giant cantilever bridge across the Forth, the greatest bridge in the world from 1890 to 1938 and the symbol of Scotland, had been deliberately over-engineered to prevent any such disaster as the Tay collapse ever happening again.

There were railway historians and researchers present at South Queensferry and aboard the two vessels in the middle of the Forth. Stories were revealed and archives unveiled. We learned that more than one and a half million trains had crossed the Forth Bridge safely since it was opened by HRH the Prince of Wales (later King Edward VII) on 1 March 1890 as the greatest engineering feat in the world. Today, some 110 trains, mostly passenger, cross it every day, compared with about ninety-five, nearly half of them freights, in 1938.

Some of the archival revelations took us back to the disaster on the Tay, ten and a half years before the Forth Bridge was completed. The seventy-five persons who died that late December night in 1879 would have been seventy-seven, but for two unexpected departures from the fated train. The exact number of passengers swept to their deaths in the Tay is known because of the recorded evidence from the station agent at St Fort, who collected the tickets, noted two season ticket holders, and left eleven other passengers with their tickets because they were travelling onwards from Dundee. Five North British employees, including the driver, fireman, and guard, were lost.

We know about many of the passengers from the careful research by journalist John Prebble whose book, *The High Girders*, was published in 1956. We know from him about William Henry Benyon who boarded the train at Ladybank and talked with another passenger in a first class compartment who left the train at Leuchars. But we shall never know the name of the man who heard a porter at Ladybank calling 'change here for Perth' and who, on the spur of the moment, decided to make his Monday calls in that city instead of going on to Dundee.

Ladybank had been a junction since the 1860s, when a line went to Perth by way of Newburgh and the banks of the Tay, while the main route led off to Leuchars and Tayport for a ferry to Dundee. Once the Tay Bridge had been opened in 1878, this route became very much the main line and the line to Perth became a North British branch. Closed for many years under the Beeching plan, it has been resuscitated by a more enlightened British Rail and carries express services to Perth although its intermediate stations remain closed.

On that December day in 1879, it unexpectedly saved the life of a passenger. He was one of the few not to have come forward at the various inquiries to give evidence.

But the most dramatic sparing of a life came at Leuchars Junction, where Mr William Linskill, a first class passenger, was literally saved by a porter's shout. Halted at Leuchars in the rising gale, with rain lashing the coaches, Mr Linskill opened the window and asked if a carriage had arrived to take him to St Andrews where a

114

friend was expecting him for the night. It had not, he was told, so he settled back on the cushions to travel on to Dundee and find a hotel, perhaps visiting St Andrews on his return journey.

The whistle blew and the guard swung his lantern but at that moment the porter who had told Mr Linskill that there was no conveyance shouted to him to alight. He banged on the window and assisted the passenger out of the train just as the engine began to pull its train into the violent night. 'Your carriage has just arrived, Sir,'were the life-saving words.

When the Forth Bridge was opened in 1890 , people were at first reluctant to travel across it, memories of the Tay Bridge disaster of eleven years before being so strong. Early passengers developed the habit of throwing a coin into the river, not only to bring good luck but to satiate the forces of nature. Among the passengers travelling later that first year was Mr William Linskill, who, it was rumoured, flung a Golden Sovereign from his purse into the estuary.

# 38

# Strange Incidents on the West Highland

QUEEN Street Station, Glasgow, regarded by the late Sir John Betjeman as the most elegant of stations with the finest Adams-style fanlight in Britain, was for decades the departure point of the 5.46am train to Fort William and Mallaig. One early morning in late steam days the train for Fort William got away with powerful exhaust beats up the tunnel bank to Cowlairs with two K4 Moguls hauling eight coaches, including a restaurant car and the sleeper from London which had been brought laboriously from Edinburgh.

It was a normal, on time, run to Fort William, with breakfast served against a backdrop of some of Scotland's finest moor and mountain scenery. Arrived at Fort William, the sleeper, restaurant car and one coach were uncoupled, as was usually the case. But departure time for the run to Mallaig came and nothing happened.

Then an elderly ex-North British 0-6-0 tender locomotive arrived from the depot and attached three coaches to the rear of the train. At last a solitary K4 Mogul came from the depot to take charge of the train.

'Eight coaches and one engine on the Mallaig extension is chancing it,' mused a railway enthusiast with knowledge of the line. But it was dry weather and the locomotive took control of its train with competence, keeping time at the various stops. All went well until the famous West Highland rain began in typical style as the train neared Beasdale. The optimists were dismayed, the pessimists aboard muttered 'told you so.'

The K4 started to slip and on the 1 in 48 bank she came gradually to a halt. An attempt to restart resulted in the train rolling backwards to the bottom of the gradient. Eventually, the train was uncoupled and the engine took the first four coaches to Arisaig, where it could run round and return for the rest of the train. The 'cognoscenti' thought back to Armagh as they sat.

Mallaig was eventually reached nearly two hours late and that was in the days when mail to the outer islands was dependent upon the train and steamers (a gale delaying MacBraynes in the Outer Hebrides was felt in London letter boxes the next day). But the ferry waited on this occasion.

On the West Highland around this period German rail-buses were being tried out, as they were on the Aberdeen-Ballater line. The unit was on the Dumbarton to Arrochar and Tarbet section.

The railbus terminated at Arrochar and Tarbet station. On a noted occasion an off-duty signalman joined it, wanting to catch a steamer at Craigendoran, and he asked the driver to 'step on it'. A vague hand-signal authorised the start, from the wrong road.

At speed the journey on the four-wheeled vehicle was more than uncomfortable but it hurtled up the 1 in 57 to Glen Douglas summit and then charged down the other side at what must have been close to 60mph. Near Whistlefield a detonator exploded immediately under the floor of the railbus and alarmed passengers. There was a sudden stop, whereupon the guard conferred with the driver. They decided it did not mean anything, so they continued to the next box. Here the signalman knew nothing about the detonator.

It was presumed at first to have been a prank, although why anyone should have travelled to such a relatively remote spot to have his fun was far from clear. In fact, after enquiries, it was found that a farmer had placed it there to protect his sheep, having discovered on recent railbus journeys at speed that they did not recognise danger from such a strange vehicle, and some had been run down.

---

DURING three summers in the late 1950s on the lines of North Wales, a mystery train was organised for senior citizens, starting in Shrewsbury. A husband and wife team ran it (he later became a Public Relations Officer for London Midland at Birmingham) and called it the 'Cambrian Radio Cruise'.

Each coach was open, with swivel armchair seating, and no one under fifty could buy a ticket. The passengers were given a commentary on their journey but never told where they were going. Such was the variety of routes still existing before Beeching that the same journey (and it was made every Wednesday) was rarely repeated.

The story is told of a would-be passenger at Shrewsbury running up to a porter and asking where the train he could see well filled was going. Only the engine carried the headboard 'Cambrian Radio Cruise'. 'I don't know,' replied the porter. 'Nobody here does. They'll tell us when it gets back.'

# 39

# Late Running

THE history of railways abounds with stories of disasters and near disasters that had timing as the great catalyst acting upon the varied ingredients of other circumstances and the intended or expected course of events for, in all activities, timing is of the essence: from the strike of a cobra to the performance of a symphony; from the baking of cake to an eclipse of the sun. And everyone can recollect at least one incident when the events of a few minutes, or even a few seconds, have held within them the tiny decisive elements that have shaped greater events to follow.

Such an occasion arose during the winter of 1931 at a small but important junction station - long since gone - situated in the Black Country, in an area which was then a depressing patchwork of pastoral and agricultural land partly destroyed by a tide of industrial developments. Some of these, too, were in decline following the Wall Street crash of 1929 but, for the most part, the local heavy industries continued as usual to cast their smoky and gloomy shadows across the landscape.

Oakbury Junction handled secondary traffic between the north-west and the junction routes south-eastwards and southwards. There was also a short single-line branch that curved south from the station before swinging back north-eastwards, under the diverging

junction lines, then up a shallow valley with an abandoned canal and some apparently derelict villages
bearing the quaintly improbable names of Ditch-
Hampry, Nitbarrow and Gompling.

Oakbury Junction station had originated in the twen-
ties as a temporary unmanned halt when a nearby
factory was being built. Two long goods loops, one each
side of the running lines, had been re-allocated as platform roads for open platforms located near to the south-
eastern end of the loops. Beyond them was a level
crossing. Later, with the completion of the factory, and
with the establishment of other industrial premises in the
area, the station had been given proper buildings and a
footbridge. Also, a bay platform had been created at the
southern corner of the station for use by the branch line
train.

Since almost all the passenger trains using the line
were stopping trains the two middle roads at Oakbury,
between the former goods loops, were often used as
goods loops and were frequently occupied by goods
trains awaiting paths.

Timing at Oakbury, as at many other stations, had its
peculiarities: for instance the branch line train - a push-
pull tank engine with one coach - was conveniently
scheduled to arrive at 4.03pm (week-days only) and then
wait for half an hour during which period two up trains
(heading southwards) and one down train would make
their two minute station stops. The timetable then indi-
cated that another down train was due to arrive at
4.33pm at exactly the booked time for the branch train to
depart form the adjoining bay platform. In practice the
departure of the branch line train was always delayed for
the odd minute or two necessary to allow for an adequate
connection interval.

The day concerned was New Year's Eve which, in
1931, fell on a Friday. Remote from any direct connections with Hogmanay celebrations Oakbury was

involved with only two temporary alterations to its section of the working timetable. Both concerned passenger trains that were to be run in two parts. One was a morning train that was to operate with the first part omitting most of the usual stops whilst the second part, following some twelve minutes later, was to make all the stops. The other alteration was to an afternoon up train. This was also due to run in two parts but with the first part booked to stop at Oakbury at the usual time of 4.15pm. However, the departure time had been extended by nine minutes to allow the second part of the train to run through on the middle up line.

Shortly after the first part arrived at the up platform a goods train drew in on the middle down line, but almost immediately it was sent forward because the two down passenger trains that would normally have preceded it were reported as running eleven minutes late.

Meanwhile the through up passenger train, with a booked passing time of 4.23pm, was similarly behind schedule. So, for nearly a quarter of an hour, whilst the up stopping train waited quietly alongside platform 2, the only sounds to be heard were those of nearby road traffic and a stationary gas engine that chugged slowly, with numerous misfiring, driving a dynamo to supply power to a small factory.

Then the level crossing gates clanged into position across the road, and the push-pull train for the branch line departed. For once, it left precisely on time.

A few moments later the expected up through train came into view, travelling fast, but headed by only a tank engine! Commonly-felt misgivings about the suitability of tank locomotives for high speed running were more than justified by the spectacle of this one, wildly blowing off steam, as it rocked and swung violently from side to side on its hurtling progress through the station at the head of a lurching van and five bogie carriages. As the last of these cleared the level crossing the locomotive,

121

with no slackening of speed, approached the junction. Here its route was to the left on a tightening curve leading to the double span bridge over the branch line and the canal.

The, just before reaching the bridge, the locomotive became derailed and, with its train, crossed the down metals, and plunged on to the push-pull train that had only just left Oakbury. At almost the same moment one of the two late running down trains, coming off the bridge, collided with the last carriage of the derailed train and, in turn, left the tracks to add to the wreckage already spread to the far side of the canal and a farm (where a strangely late-running gathering of the harvest had not yet reached completion).

Timing, in this instance, could not have prevented the original derailment, but adherence to the working timetable would have prevented the branch line train from being involved, and it just could have allowed time for the down train to have been stopped before reaching the bridge.

As things turned out, the damage resulting from the accident was mainly what would now be described as environmental, with a considerable amount of landscaping being required. The Bowman tank engine that was the prime cause of the accident was found to be undamaged, and was back in service after a few days. The Bassett-Lowke 4-6-0 tender engine of the Down train suffered several scratches and some minor dents. One of the luxury first class corridor bogie carriages (each acquired at the cost of 400 BDV cigarette coupons) had its buffers bent and its couplings twisted.

Mercifully the only casualty was a lead brown-and-white bull. It had been decapitated.

# 40

# The Train That Took the Plunge

THE first railway in the Channel Islands was not in Jersey, where a veritable 'network' was built up early this century, but on much smaller Alderney. In fact, construction of the line goes back to 1847, with the intention of carrying rock from an old quarry owned by the Admiralty to the harbour.

There were no shareholders, the tracks and rolling stock, locomotive and general machinery were owned by the Admiralty, while the land on which the line was laid belonged to the War Office. It was only two miles long, but laid to standard gauge, although it served no real passenger purpose. The Islanders used it, though, travelling in wagons, proud that Alderney should possess such a technological achievement.

A royal visit by Queen Victoria and Prince Albert took place in Augus 1854, when the Royal Yacht dropped anchor in Braye Bay. The royal couple were brought ashore accompanied by their aides, and let to the first - and only - royal 'coach' on the railway, a converted wagon painted pink with soft chairs installed under a calico-hung roof. Various local dignataries travelled in more customary style in open wagons behind the royal party.

Starting at 9.20 in the morning the train chuffed along the rough track and reached the quarry in fifteen minutes. It is not clear how they emerged from that destination to undertake official engagements in the tiny capital town of St Anne, but their return to the fortified harbour of Braye Bay was not by train.

Curiously, Alderney, with only three square miles, still has a railway, the only one in the Channel Islands. The Jersey Central and Jersey Eastern systems are but memories, and even in Guernsey the buses (now mostly owned by Chelsea Football Club) no longer carry the wording 'Guernsey Railway Company'. But from Braye Road to the quarry a diesel called *Molly* and an industrial steam tank engine provide an every half hour service for tourists during the long season. The diesel does some off-season work moving rock to the breadwater, which is now the responsibility of the Department of the Environment.

Trinity House and the Admiralty became involved some eighty years ago when the Peckett steam locomotive and its train became 'a menace to shipping'.

There was by all reports a fierce storm raging on the afternoon on 28 November 1911 when the locomotive was hauling a rock train from the quarry to the breakwater. Waves were breaking over the track and seaweed was being washed over the lines, while the spray was so bad the driver could not see through his oblong cab windows. Hanging out, he noticed that the train was nearing the end of the breakwater and his efforts to stop were to no avail on the wet and greasy track.

At a speed of nearly 20mph the driver and his mate jumped for their lives, landing hard on the edge of the breakwater. The engine and her whole train plunged into the sea, becoming a danger to navigation! These are dangerous waters due to the tidal race through the Swinge Channel, and the presence of the train in shallow water actually worsened it in certain conditions of wind and tide. It was dredged up in a ruined state about six months later and then scrapped, but as the Alderney Railway actually operated at a profit, the engine and rolling stock were replaced.

Unlike their work with defensive railway construction on Jersey, the occupying German forces had no use for the Alderney Railway which became theirs after June, 1940. The line remained intact, to be cleared and re-opened in the late 1970's under the auspices of the Alderney Railway Society (a remarkable body considering that only 1600 people live on the island) and began running again in April, 1980, with the diesel *Molly*. There are now very sturdy buffers on the breakwater.

# 41

---

# Saturday Night
# Manouevres

---

BETWEEN Lakenheath and Thetford, on the line from Ely to Norwich, there is an extensive area of heathland used by the army. Many of the episodes of the popular television series *Dad's Army* were filmed in this region, although the preserved North Norfolk Railway was the venue for train scenes, especially Weybourne (pronounced locally as 'Webburn') Station.

Brandon is the still active station before Thetford, where several sidings house military trains. Late on a Saturday night in the summer of 1975, one such train consisting of a diesel locomotive and a set of Mark 1 coaches was due to come along the line from Cambridge and to be attacked as part of army manoeuvres, a 'no holds barred' operation involving time-expired rolling stock.

On that particular night engineering works had begun on the line closer to London, and these delayed the scheduled 2306 train from Liverpool Street to Norwich via Ely. In fact it was an hour late approaching Brandon where the regular signalman had gone off-shift, replaced by a special man to handle military traffic. The inevitable happened - the 2306 passed through Brandon and then swung into a siding. The alarmed driver stopped his train well short of the siding limit and, cursing, got down from his cab to check with the box. It was quite a walk back along the track to the lighted box, and as he was trudging angrily towards it, some 300 soldiers burst out from cover and hurled themselves at the stationary train!

The soldiery was fearsome, with blackened faces and wearing twigs and other bits of greenery, brandishing rifles and bayonets. Immediately they seized the unfortunate driver, tying hands behind his back and gagging him. Postal workers in the van at the rear of the train shook with terror, believing this to be the 'Second Great Train Robbery' with a bigger gang than in 1962. Passengers suffered even more, as windows were smashed, shouting men invading the compartments and dragging them out. Many of the riders were, as usual on a Saturday night, late theatregoers returning to Norfolk. Perhaps the women on board startled the soldiery for they were handled less roughly but still bundled out of the train. Cries and protests were ignored; the men on manoeuvres had been told to expect them from the 'civvy-soldiers' on the train.

On Brandon Station a horrified Mr Basil Hyatt, inspector in charge of the railway operation, ran towards the Commanding Officer but before he could reach him he, too, was pounced upon and arrested. Somehow he convinced his captors that something had gone terribly wrong and he was taken to the CO. But that officer, despite whistles, firing of guns in the air by his subordinates, and much shouting, found it difficult to stop the attack. It took all of another five minutes to call it off, and by that time the 2306 from Liverpool Street - although still on the track - was unfit for further passenger use.

And all the time the real military train, with its condemned rake of coaches, waited at Ely for a green light.

The affair was hushed up for years. Passengers were taken onwards in army transport, and mail in an army lorry. Compensation was paid to the Eastern Region, as it was then, for some twenty smashed windows, two stove-in doors, damaged upholstery and broken lights.

# 42

# Change
# for Denbigh Hall

COMPLETION of the London and Birmingham Railway, which opened throughout in October 1838, was held up by heavy works between Wolverton and Rugby, especially the drilling of Kilsby Tunnel, 2423yds long. For nearly a year there was a road gap requiring connection by stage coaches over some thirty miles.

Trains from Euston terminated at a temporary station named Denbigh Hall, and trains from Birmingham halted at Rugby. In normal circumstances, three stage coaches managed the intervening road journey in under three hours, cantering along rather roughly at an average speed of 11mph, first class passengers seated inside and second class on top.

All too often, however, there was insufficient space for the sort of heavy luggage taken by travellers in those days, and this had to be stowed in a cart or omnibus, which took a good deal longer than the stages. Confusion, even chaos, was the order of the day at both ends of the line with lost tickets and misplaced or damaged luggage items commonplace.

A major event occurred during the summer of 1838 which imposed appalling strain upon the primitive transfer arrangements. Queen Victoria's Coronation caused heavy bookings from Birmingham, but so far as the London and Birmingham Railway was concerned, according to a historian, any number of passengers could be conveyed by their trains. The road gap was quite a different matter. The railway could contract only a few coaches, but did not inform London-bound travellers that there could be a problem.

On the 'middle ground', as it was called, the London and Birmingham did not hold itself responsible for bookings beyond the three contracted stage coaches. When hundreds of people poured off trains at Rugby, clutching tickets to Euston, they were confronted with touts offering seats in omnibuses, carts, and even donkey chaises at prices from £10 to £20, the latter price being the equivalent to a workman's annual wage.

A Mr and Mrs Jackson, from a village near Birmingham, were travelling to London to attend the Coronation and were looking forward to their first ride on a train. They did indeed enjoy the experience, commenting favourably upon the smoothness and speed, sometimes exceeding 30mph, which enabled them to reach the 'little town of Rugby' in not much more than an hour, including a stop at the ancient city of Coventry.

Alighting with a crowd of other passengers, probably more than a hundred strong, they encountered horrifying confusion. Their tickets were not honoured on the three stage coaches, which quickly galloped away with sixteen or seventeen people loaded, some on top clinging to heavy leather bags. Threats, shouts, noise so confused them that eventually they had to resort to a donkey-chaise for which they parted with £10, a sum greatly in excess of their return tickets form Birmingham to London in second class rail accommodation.

A weary donkey ambled along the rough road with stops for rest, and rain showers contributed to their misery. Their baggage was piled upon their laps, and no food or refreshment could be obtained along the way.

They spoke 'perpetually of the contrast between the old form of transport and the new which they had so briefly sampled'. No doubt they looked forward to reaching Denbigh Hall and the comfort (and warmth) of a train more than anyone had - or has since.

What they expected to find at the proudly named Denbigh Hall Temporary Terminus is not known, but what they did find is well documented. There was a bridge, new and quite elegant. There was a wooden platform. On the road leading up to it there was a great deal of mud and many horses and carts, stacked luggage and some rough-looking carriers. Across the road was an 'insignificant inn' which gloried in the name 'Denbigh Hall'. Apart from a hut on the 'station' platform and another hut beside the road, in which hauliers gathered, there were no other buildings.

A railway servant told them, in gathering darkness, that the next train was not coming until four in the morning, mainly for third class in open trucks behind the Royal Mail. They were advised to try and take a room at the inn and catch the eight o'clock for Euston.

The Jacksons tried the inn, and were told it was full but they could have a couch in the parlour. It seems that 'Denbigh Hall' owed its name to the Earl of Denbigh, who was travelling years previously with his coach and four on a severe winter's night and had been forced to seek lodging in an 'obscure dwelling', the residence of one Moll Harris, an old and apparently very ignorant woman. The Earl was delighted by the warmth, comfort and hospitality afforded him, and when leaving two days later, asked for a bill. Mill Harris handed him a hatchet, not knowing any other meaning of the word. The Earl paid handsomely for the hatchet, which he kept as a momento, and added what was a lot of money for the late eighteenth century for his room and board. The old woman renamed the place 'Denbigh Hall' and eventually two or three rooms were added.

It became quite famous on the road to Holyhead and other places in the north west, so that when the London and Birmingham Railway come on the scene it named the bridge after it and the long cutting (from which over a million cubic yards of earth were removed). The bridge still stands, carrying the railway over the A5 road to Holyhead, between Bletchley and Wolverton, and close to the modern sprawl of Milton Keynes. It is a dual carriage way road now and the bridge had to be structurally altered and extended. Few know it as Denbigh Hall, and of the 'insignificant inn' there is no trace remaining.

When the Jacksons reached Euston next morning soon after ten o'clock, they were well pleased with their train ride but aghast at the cost of the 'middle ground', which had been five times the price of their railway ticket plus five shillings for their night's lodging. It made an unexpected hole in their finances and forced an early return to Birmingham after Queen Victoria's Coronation. History does not record if they were successful in gaining accommodation on a connecting contracted carriage across the 'middle ground'.

Historians frequently record the speed and comfort of trains compared to the days of the stage coaches, but they do not often mention two other very important factors. The trains carried far more people, up to twenty times as many on an express (and in some instances such as the 40 coach excursions to Brighton and elsewhere sometimes fifty times) the number a horse-drawn stage could accommodate. The cost, too, was much lower. This was discovered by travellers going to Cornwall as late as the 1850s, before Brunel's Royal Albert Bridge was built. The fare to Plymouth from London was £5 in first class, £3 in second, but the onward ride of sixty-five miles to Falmouth in a coach and four was £6, or a hired chaise £8.

# 43

# On the Underground

THEY still tell the story of the burglar who broke into 23 Leinster Gardens, Kensington. Every time keen Sherlock Holmes readers turn to the Canon for the 'Bruce Partington Plans' they cannot help but think of the incident.

In both cases there was a body on the top of an Inner Circle train. The flat-roofed Victorian coaching stock carried them quite a distance.

The burglar, of course, must have been someone not at all familiar with the district. He found no one at home and smashed the door down with his shoulder, only to go right through the false facade and fall 40ft on to a passing train.

He lived long enough to learn of the environmental work done by the Metropolitan District system on the false-fronted houses of Kensington!

It happened, they say, most New Year's Eves close to midnight on the Central Line near Ealing in London. An eye witness on the tube, just as 1974 was drawing to its close, reported that he was sitting in a carriage with about a dozen other riders when a young lady suddenly rose to her feet.

The train had left West Acton and its next stop in two

minutes time would be Ealing Broadway, the end of the line.

The lady passenger quickly and dramatically removed her clothes and paraded naked apart from shoes once up and down her section of the carriage. Ten of the other passengers looked up but took no notice at all. The minority were aghast. Just as quickly, the lady threw on her clothes, gathered up her bag, and alighted as the doors opened at the final stop.

Our eye witness, flabergasted, asked his nearest neighbour why he had taken no notice, and indeed why most of the passengers had neither said nor done nothing. 'She does this every year' was the muttered reply.

This curious event was taken up for an advertisement in the mid-seventies. But the 'stripper' never rode the train again after New Year's Eve, 1975, or if she did, she kept her clothes on.

London's first tube railway was not the City and South London line from King William Street (Bank) to Stockwell, opened in 1890. The very first, and indeed the first anywhere in the world, was the cable-operated tube from Tooley Street to Tower Hill, just under a mile in length. This was ready for traffic in 1883, carrying passengers from a point close to London Bridge Station under the Thames to the eastern part of the city. It would be useful even today.

But the tiny passenger cars deep below ground seem to have brought on claustrophobia and dementia. One apparently normal middle-aged man suddenly went berserk as the journey began and tried to strangle the people seated on either side of him. On other trips there were people who screamed the whole time the car was in motion. The ride became deeply unpopular and the system closed down in 1885, the tube itself being used as a pedestrian tunnel until the Tower Bridge was opened in 1894. The Tower Bridge in those days was opened almost continuously in the early mornings but people could and did use the high walkway. That, however, became the haunt of madmen and prostitutes and was closed in 1909. It seems the people of southeast London by the river were doomed to make the long detour via London Bridge and Monument to reach the Mark Lane/Tower area. The Tower Bridge Walkway was re-opened in 1982, under supervision and as a tourist attraction.

Meanwhile, London's first tube was put to another use as soon as it was closed to pedestrians. The pipes of the London Hydraulic Power Company were laid through it, serving to work the thousands of lifts which at the turn of the century relied on this system. Apart from museum pieces specially retained, these lifts had ceased by 1975, but the pipes still remain under the Thames, sharing their tube space with telephone cables.

The Glasgow cable subway opened throughout on its circular route in December 1896, only to be closed by a first day crash which kept it shut for nearly a month. But it became a great success later and by the turn of the century it was carrying over twenty million people a year.

A curious legend developed about the Glasgow underground which persisted right through the early 1900s. Its atmosphere was reputed to cure whooping cough! Even some medical people agreed that a combination of the tar covering the cable and the creosote covering the wooden sleepers and platforms helped breathing.

Passengers would sometimes see parents standing on a platform holding a sickly child with a binder round its middle. Occasionally the unfortunate child would break into uncontrollable whooping. This was, of course, a very serious disease in those days and the underground staff, aware of the legend, would turn a blind eye on the presence of the invalid and its parents (provided they had paid the minimum fare of tuppence halfpenny) for as long as twelve hours.

Glasgow's cable underground, which was completely

modernised and electrified in 1980, had more ghosts on the system than any other rail network. According to Gordon Casely and Bill Hamilton, who wrote a book called *I Belong to Glasgow* in 1975, there were two regular ghosts but 'sightings' of half a dozen more were frequent occurrences.

There were men working for the underground whose job it was to walk the thirteen miles of the circle after the last trains had stopped running. They were looking for broken rails, flooding (one workmen found an 18in eel swimming about in a watery sump), and any other untoward problems which could affect the early morning start-up.

Most famous of the ghosts is the 'Grey Lady'. She has been 'seen and heard' near Shields Road station, and is reputed to be an unfortunate lady passenger who fell with her tiny daughter in front of a train at Shields Road in 1922. Station staff just managed to save the child but the lady was killed. In the small hours of the morning she is said to roam the track and two cleaners claim to have seen her, while several others have heard her crying.

Two separate squads of men were working on the track one night when a light was spotted between them. On investigation nothing was found, but one of them later saw a middle aged man in a raincoat and flat cap. He told the man to follow him along the track to the Broomloan Road exit to the open, and heard the man's footsteps behind him, but on reaching the exit he looked back and there was no one there.

A rigger at the underground sheds saw the figure of a man in the driver's cab of an empty train. He went over to talk with him, but when he climbed in, there was only a freezing chill in the compartment. Two of the rigger's colleagues had this experience a few days later.

London's deep level tubes have their share of ghosts, not surprisingly since they date back to the late Victorian era.

One station on the busy Central Line has been closed since 1915. This was Museum, between Holborn Kingsway and Tottenham Court Road, an original stop on the 'Tuppenny Tube' from Liverpool Street to Shepherd's Bush, opened in 1900.

The exits from Museum led up to the British Museum, the twisting metal staircase for emergency purposes passing within a few feet of the chilly underground chamber in which the largest collection of Egyptian mummies were kept outside Cairo.

Used as a shelter for people in London seeking refuge from aerial attacks, first by Zeppelins and later by Gotha bombers, the station was busy in the days (and nights) of World War I, but trains did not stop. It later became a storage depot for Government files and archives and other semi-secret material, entered only by authorised civil servants.

Central Line trains rumbled through quite slowly between the wars, the tiled outlines of the station being clearly visible to passengers. Very occasionally, people were seen on the platform when travelling westbound, but they were not passengers. Apart form a short hoot, drivers paid no attention to them. But Driver Morley, taking his Ealing train through slowly in the autumn of 1938, was startled to see a completely bandaged figure standing near the tunnel mouth. Alarmed, he brought his train to a stop, and switched on his cab lights to maximum. The mummy - for that was what it seemed to be - stood there unmoving. Morley left his cab and entered the passenger compartment of the first coach, blurting out what he had seen. 'Look at it - look through your windows,' he yelled. Several passengers did so but saw only the empty, disused platform.

On what was originally the Euston and Hampstead Tube, later the Morden-Edgware Line, and now the Northern Line, there was a station next to Hampstead called 'Bull and Bush'. It served a famous public house on the heath and, of course, the recreation areas around it. But it was never completed and only a few passengers managed to use it from 1907 to 1908. The sheer depth of the line at this point, 350ft below the level of the heath, was against it, many people preferring to walk from Golders Green or take a horse omnibus up the hill. Nevertheless, unconfirmed reports of singing, costumed groups on the supposedly blocked-off platforms continued up to the start of World War I.

# 44

# 'Carrying On'

REGULAR travellers to Kent by Network Southeast services are accustomed to delays, cancellations, and excuses ranging from signal and points failures to leaves on the line. While one has a good deal of sympathy with those whose job it is to keep the trains running without the larger and more dedicated staff of yesteryear, some of the reasons for lateness or the total non-arrival of trains pale beside the effort of the Southern Railway Company and its committed work force back in the summer and autumn of 1940.

Kent was a perpetual target of bombers for months on end, and it also suffered from crashing aircraft, both British and German, some of which fell on stations and railway lines.

Perhaps the story of Southern Railway motorman Freddy Smith might make present day staff look more closely at their own conditions. He was on the Victoria to Maidstone East service and on the second Friday in October, 1940, his Maidstone home had been bombed. Driver Smith was blown head first from his front door into the paint shop across the road. Although his sister was injured in the wrecked house, he only suffered a bump on the head and reported for duty next day.

On the Monday he had taken a train to Victoria and was returning to Maidstone with the 5.20pm. The line had only been electrified for about eighteen months. Shortly after leaving the terminus in the rapidly darkening evening, anti-aircraft guns opened up around Battersea, and in his words 'they rocked the train something awful'. However, the run to Bromley South was uneventful, but heading eastwards from that station bombs were dropped by the side of the wall close to Bickley, the next station. He was not due to stop there and passed through, accelerating. But the glass on the station roof fell in and some of the windows of the train were broken. The driver 'heard some squeals' as he looked back out of the window. However, all seemed reasonably well so he carried on to the next stop, at Swanley Junction. Just as he was slowing for it, a Molotov 'bread-basket' fell in front of the train and spread across the rails 'lighting the night like day'.

Undeterred, the driver held the train at Swanley for a couple of minutes while people from the coach with the shattered windows moved through into the third one from the front. It was as well they did, for another incendiary went through the roof of the empty coach as they took the junction towards Otford. The fire was only small and the guard put it out.

A girl with a baby came and asked if she could ride in the cab. She said she was scared stiff. 'So am I,' replied Driver Smith, but he let her in.

On the way down Wrotham bank, travelling at 60mph the train was again rocked, either by nearby gunfire or by bombs. But the battered train arrived intact at Maidstone East. A *Kent Messenger* reporter was on the platform and interviewed the driver, who simply replied that he was only doing his job and regretted that he had arrived *ten minutes late*!

NEARLY every railway station in Kent had a story to tell of the Battle of Britain, and the *Kent Messenger* newspaper was on the trail of all of them. One incident at Whitstable caused by a stick of bombs hitting the track resulted in an emergency bus service, quickly provided by the East Kent Company, but as the railway authorities in the region pointed out, the down line was rapidly reinstated and buses were withdrawn *after five hours!*

There was a temporary porter named George Garrett working at Herne Hill. On 8 November 1940 he was flagging trains by hand as the signals had been destroyed by bombs the day before. However, just as an electric train had gone past him bombs fell. He heard them whistling down and flung himself flat on the track, fortunately missing the conductor rail. But the explosions lifted him bodily on to the up platform then carried him forward by suction to the junction with the Loughborough line. Dazed, he struggled to his feet, finding that he was covered in rags. Apparently, under the tracks there had been a rag merchant's store.

Trains coming from Blackfriars and Holborn Viaduct were delayed for four hours, but George carried on flag signalling those coming from Victoria, then had to lie up for a few days in delayed shock. Yardmaster W. G. K. Dorne, who was in charge at Herne Hill throughout the Blitz, commented that 'We marry the Railway and become part of it body and soul.' George Garrett, soon confirmed in the job, did just that.

On an August day in 1982 there was a fire in a junction box controlling signal wires between London Bridge and New Cross on the Network Southeast lines to Kent. No trains ran for twenty-four hours and no hand signalling was attempted.

Arriving at Liverpool Street Station shortly after one o'clock in the afternoon of Saturday, 8 June 1991 I emerged from the tube to see a large placard. This stated that due to the wires being down near Chadwell Heath there were no trains running on the main Great Eastern line. The Boat Train to Harwich for the Scandinavian Seaways ship to Hamburg, which I was planning to join, would be replaced by buses, which were now waiting by the top of the steps beyond the shopping mall.

It would not be correct to say that this was unexpected, as it would have been thirty years ago. Sadly, one must now expect the unexpected. Although only four stoppages had affected my travels in the period, there had been wires down or blocked tracks - or - on 30 April 1991 a total cessation of services from Liverpool Street due to a fire in Bishopsgate not even touching the station. Altogether, there were seventeen occasions in the year with traffic disruption on the lines from Liverpool Street.

The London and North Eastern Railway in East Anglia was the target for much bombing in 1940-41 and again in 1944. During this time the railways of the region handled twenty-five times their pre-war tonnages. For four months from April 1943, three quarters of a million tons of rubble from London and Essex bombed sites were taken to East Anglia for American aerodrome construction by 1700 extra trains, and 167,000 personnel were carried by passenger trains to those airfields.

The lines and structural points ranging from bridges to signal boxes between Liverpool Street and Chelmsford and between Bethnal Green and Bishops Stortford were damaged by more than 3000 bombs. The very first V1 'Flying Bomb' fell on a signal box on the Southern Railway near Cuckfield in Sussex, without causing any traffic interuption. The second V1 of the war was more serious; it fell on the LNERs four-track bridge over Grove Road near Stratford and damage was colossal. It took four days to restore trains over the bridge, during which time trains were diverted to Fenchurch Street or began their journeys form Stratford Station. This was the longest period that Liverpool Street was partly out of action (trains on the Cambridge line being able to run). There were six occasions during the entire war when no trains at all were able to use Liverpool Street for periods ranging from three hours to one and a half days.

Liverpool Street's grimy spires and wondrous filigrees are pristine now ('What giant race of men built these marvels?' muses a visitor from the twenty-fifth century in the ode) but too often they look down on inactivity below.

# 45

# Highland Railway Surprise

THE Highland Railway built its line to the far north, financed to the tune of £60,000 by the Third Duke of Sutherland. It wound its way up Strath Kildonan and then across the wilderness of the Caithness Flow Country, traversing many roadless miles. There are just tracks, still to Aultnabreac and Scotscalder stations, and not until a train reaches Georgemas Junction, Britain's most northerly railway divide, is an 'A' road encountered, leading from Wick to Thurso.

Modernisation has come to the far north lines with Sprinters coupled together, which split at Georgemas, one two-coach unit (happily these days always well filled) going to Thurso and the other to Wick. Standing passengers are not all that rare especially those with massive back-packs, on summer services, and while locals may not use their lifeline all that much, they welcome the trains with cheery waves.

On a Saturday morning early in May, 1991, two crofters, standing beside their horses after some work close to the tree plantations - those controversial investments which are changing the character of the wild Flow Country - heard the roar of an approaching diesel. It was quite a bit earlier than the first Sprinter train of the day should have been, and they stared in some surprise towards the source of the sound. What they saw was unexpected in the extreme.

The longest and clearly the most luxurious train ever to run over these remote miles was heading north, winding its way past Altnabreac. One Class 37 diesel engine was noisily but effectively coping with the heavy load of seventeen coaches. The train consisted of eight day coaches with white roofs and 'raspberry ripple' colours on the sides, pretty Pullman-style lamps lit at every table, two clearly marked kitchen cars, and a string of seven ultra-modern sleeping cars.

Many dozens of passengers after finishing their hearty breakfasts, happily returned the waves of the puzzled onlookers. Neither of the two men were old enough to remember the last time a somewhat similar though shorter and less well-equiped train had passed over these tracks. That was on Sunday (Sunday of all days) 3 August 1941, when a special conveying the then Mr Winston Churchill and his entourage, plus a number of Naval Officers and some selected journalists, travelled from Euston to Thurso. The Prime Minister and all the other passengers were bound for Scapa Flow to embark in HMS *Prince of Wales* to meet President Roosevelt off Newfoundland and sign the Atlantic Charter.

Probably not even the crofters' fathers could have remembered the only other time a luxurious train with sleeping cars had come up the line. That was in June, 1916, and it was conveying Lord Kitchener and his staff for his ill-fated voyage to Russia aboard HMS *Hampshire*. That train returned in sections with some senior naval officers aboard, but Kitchiner's ticket perforce, had been one way only.

The 'Jellicoe Specials' had often travelled to Thurso during World War I; long and – for the period – heavy trains but without sleepers even if there were special highland saloons for senior navy staff. There is a plaque on Dingwall station in Easter Ross, were they all stopped, showing that some 136,000 cups of tea had been given to servicemen aboard the specials.

But the magnificent spectacle of May 1991 was not carrying grandees, nor even political leaders on vital missions. The passengers on that bright spring morning were on an InterCity land cruise, the first to bring its sleeping cars to the far north. These were stationed at Georgemas junction while passengers went in motor coaches to John O'Groats, where they embarked on the pedestrian ferry to Burwick on Orkney for a tour. This train was the *Orcadian* and its success led to a repeat trip every two weeks for the summer and autumn.

Inter City Land Cruises have revived the London and North Eastern Railway's *Northern Belle* cruise train of the 1930s which wandered for a week with its Pullmans and sleepers over LNER metals in Scotland. The far north was LMS territory, so it never went beyond former Great North of Scotland tracks. Lasting three or four days, the Inter City Land Cruises are becoming familiar sights in the Highlands, as the *West Highlander*, *The Highlander* and the *Sound of Sleat*, but the first *Orcadian* was a surprise to the few watchers in Sutherland and Caithness.

# 46

# Sir Nigel Gresley

THE last year of high performance steam on the Great Northern division of British Railways was 1963, when most Leeds trains and a few to Newcastle and Hull were still handled by Pacifics. The best of the Gresley A4 streamliners had already been sent to Scotland where they took over Glasgow (Buchanan Street) to Aberdeen via Perth and Forfar duties. Except for the very best one No 60007, *Sir Nigel Gresley*.

On 8 May 1963, a wet and chilly day with greasy rails and a strong southwesterly wind, I was permitted a footplate ride with 60007, joining her at Doncaster after a rather mundane ride behind a diesel from King's Cross (its poor running 'explained' at Doncaster by a young official saying 'this train is still operating to steam timings').

*Sir Nigel Gresley* came in from Leeds at the head of the *White Rose*, a train of some 400 gross tons, well laden, but twelve minutes late due to a delay at Wakefield. I clambered up into the cab accompanied by Mr Fred Hart, who had been a famous 'Top Link' driver and was in 1963 the Chief Motive Power Inspector. We joined Driver Arthur Pearce and Fireman Arthur Morris, both of Copley Hill Shed at Leeds. They were among the last generation of dedicated steam men, but even then they were having to work on diesels from time to time. They were aware of the greater creature comforts on the oil-powered monsters but greatly regretted the individualism, the team effort, that went into making a 'Top Link' steam run.

External circumstances permitting, they were going to strive for a memorable run non-stop to London, and in this they had Fred Hart's approval, and obviously mine. The schedule looks, today, very slow, allowing 165 minutes for the 156 miles, but the tracks had not then been up graded for high speed running later associated with high speed trains, while the length and weight of the popular *White Rose* was greater than is normally found today.

There were no external delays on the run, not even a permanent way slack outside of the usual ones, such as through Peterborough, limited to 20mph. *Sir Nigel Gresley* was given her head, and steam pressure was kept up fully the whole time, both Fred Hart and myself taking some turns with the shovel (I put on at least a quarter of a ton of coal, not, perhaps, in the most skilful manner but at least it went in to the hungry maw). After breasting Stoke Summit speed built up to a breathless figure, only Fred Hart checking it against quarter mile posts accurately.

Thsi was, of course, the famous LNER racing ground where *Mallard* in 1938 had attained 126mph to secure, probably for all time, the world record with steam traction, albeit downhill, a point consistently made to this day by the Germans, whose locomotive hauling the *Vliegende Hamburger* in 1938 had achieved 124.5mph on level track.

I was absolutely sure we had exceeded 100mph by Essendine, and at that point, with the engine still accelerating, all four of us saw the white wind-whipped steam forming features above us. Were they those, we wondered, of Sir Nigel himself, looking down from some railway Valhalla on his namesake locomotive, which still proudly demonstrated - after a quarter of a century - his brilliant designing skill combining power and appearence?

We came into King's Cross a minute early, having gained thirteen minutes on the run from Doncaster. Surprisingly, and unexpectedly, there was a welcoming committee, with the divisional manager, the station master (in tradition silk hat) a public relations official, and one or two others. Photographs were taken of all of us grouped around the locomotive.

'When you write about this journey please remember that the maximum allowed speed is 90mph', I was told.' For the time being, do not mention the maximum that we actually did.' 'And what was that?' I asked. 'Fully 107mph' replied Fred Hart, who kept the log and regarded it as one of the best runs he had ever ridden.

A few weeks later, 60007 headed a railway enthusiasts' special and came down Stoke Bank at 108mph. I received a short letter from Fred Hart in which he said 'Now you may tell your readers what we did on our run.'

# 47

# 'Following Close Behind'

THE main line from Aberdeen to Glasgow by way of Forfar and Perth was steam worked from 1962 to 1966, using Gresley's A4 streamliners aided by some Stanier Black Fives. Curiously, it had been diesel-worked from the mid 1950s by North British Locomotive Company Type 2 engines, but these had proved a sad disaster, averaging failures on the track at least one trip in four. 'Steam Still Scores' was the headline of the press release put out by BR Scottish Region when the A4s came to the rescue.

Schedules were set at three hours for the 153 difficult miles, with stops at Stonehaven, Forfar, Perth, Gleneagles and Stirling. Some magnificent runs were achieved, with comparatively light trains, except for the morning and evening business expresses with their restaurant cars. The route never went back to diesel working, for it was closed between Kinnaber Junction through Forfar to Perth under the legacy of the Beeching cuts. Trains were diverted via Dundee and Montrose.

On a brilliantly sunny day in May, 1965, several members of the Fleet Street Railway Circle, then touring in the Highlands, came to Aberdeen, and were offered a ride on the 5.15pm semi-fast to Perth, which followed the 5pm express. The locomotive rostered for the 5pm, A4 No 60024, *Kingfisher*, was replaced by a Black Five and the 5.15pm given the streamliner. I was a member of the half dozen writers riding this train, and we were allowed on the footplate two at a time. *Kingfisher* gleamed in the afternoon sunlight, much time and effort having been expended by Ferryhill Shed to get her in this condition.

My turn on the crowded footplate was from Stonehaven to Laurencekirk, a station now long gone on the dismantled main line. The chief inspector from Aberdeen decided to drive and sent the actual driver back into the train to get a cup of tea. This left only four on the footplate, where we had a wild ride, holding 82mph for several miles on track where the maximum was 75.

The unexpected came at Forfar, where we approached the station twenty two minutes ahead of time, with the 5pm express only then drawing out. The last 32½ miles on to Perth took just thirty minutes, and they put us into a terminating bay while the 5pm was still in the station!

Brigadier W G Thorpe, then general manager of the Scottish Region, waved his magic wand to make this experience possible. He expected, so he said, all kind of official recriminations from on high for his desire to show off his A4s. Instead, he was made deputy chairman of the British Railways Board.

# 48

---

# A Death Throes Spasm
# on the
# Great North of Ireland

---

BY 1962 the Great North of Ireland Railway, the Great Northern (I) as it was known, had been pronounced well and truly dead. No longer would its handsome blue engines be seen pounding out of Belfast's Great Victoria Street on the way to Londonderry via Omagh, or to Newcastle, or on the main line to Dublin. Here was a case of a railway ending the war in an amazingly profitable state from all its six years of heavy haulage, favoured - as the railways of Southern Ireland were not - with an allocation of decent coal.

It was a railway which ran all known forms of traction in its time - steam, diesel, petrol, electric, battery and even horse (the famous Fintona Tram). It never had greater power than its fleet of 4-4-0s, but among the best and most powerful of that wheel arrangement, laid down in the rich aftermath of the war.

By 1948 the net profit had fallen to £248,000, in 1949 to £36,000 and after that the losses mounted. Nothing had been put into reserve and massive dividends had been paid during the fat years. The railway passed away, taken over jointly by Ireland's CIE and the anti-rail

Government of Northern Ireland.

But in November, 1963, on a bright mild day, I was with a couple of colleagues looking around Adelaide Shed, Belfast, which was full of interesting steam engines at that time, 'Jeep'2-6-2 tanks working suburban services, powerful Moguls on some of the stopping trains to Londonderry by both then existing routes, and a few 4-4-0s running to Dublin. Two of the pseudo-Schools were there, too, unnamed, and last used on Rugby specials to Dublin. They looked tired and dirty, a trace of blue showing.

The shedmaster, inspired by the interest being shown, suddenly had an idea. 'Be at Great Victoria Street tomorrow morning and catch the 9.50am to Portadown. I'll arrange for you to be up with the driver. You may get a surprise.'

In good time we were at the terminus (as it was then) and our train backed in slowly. It was just three coaches, but pushing it towards the buffers was a glistening engine, none other than No 7, which we had seen the day before. Someone had slapped old Great Northern paint on her, and built wooden nameplates, *Boyne*, outlined in gold. We climbed aboard the spacious cab, and uphill we went, making all the stops to Portadown and probably not exceeding 40mph at any stage, but heads turned on platforms and there were trackside waves. The old Great Northern had kicked at the roof of its coffin.

# 49

# Rude Awakenings
# on Trains

I always enjoyed my travels with Bill Simpson, that remarkable man who was head of public relations for British European Airways for so many years. Bill, of course, was one of Sir Archibald MacIndoe's 'Guinea-pigs' from the East Grinstead Hospital, where his terrible wartime aircraft burns were made acceptable. He wrote a famous book about his experiences, called *I Burned My Fingers*.

William Simpson, OBE, had been a 'victim' of the BBC television programme *This is your Life*. On it he said that air travel still appealed to him but that he also enjoyed travelling by train. While I must have made some twenty flights with Bill, I also rode four or five trains with him, twice in sleeping cars. Both of those had their share of the totally unexpected.

On a mild evening in March, 1969, several of us boarded the then Stranraer mail and sleeping car train for the overnight journey to that distant Galloway terminus. The direct route from Dumfries to Stranraer via Castle Douglas had already been torn up under the Beeching Butchery, and the train needed to travel north west to Ayr and then southwards.

Bill Simpson and I were among invited guests on a

special Scottish editorial tour, and the numbers required an extra sleeper. It was thus a heavier than usual formation which set off up the steep Girvan bank, and I awoke to the sound of excessive snarling from up-front as the diesel laboured under the load. As I threw a raincoat over my pyjamas the diesel's unhealthy roar spluttered and quietened. There were several jerks and then the train began rolling backwards.

The 1 in 54 up to the tunnel at the summit near Pinmore had proved too much for the locomotive. We rolled astern at a controlled speed towards Girvan station. As I opened the door of my sleeper, Bill Simpson was there, in his pyjamas. 'Should I be alarmed,' he asked mildly, 'or is this a controlled stall?' It was, and after about half an hour stationary at Girvan, another diesel had been found and attached to the rear of the train, which stayed with us after a second - this time successful - assault on the 1 in 54 and subsequent 1 in 67 up past Barrhill to the line's second summit. We reached Stranraer about forty-five minutes late, but for those bound for Larne by ferry there were no worries as the boat waited.

Bill Simpson recalled the previous occasion he and I had met outside our sleeper cabins in pyjamas. It was twelve years previously, in far-off Serbia.

Yugoslavia under Marshall Tito was pulling itself up by its bootlaces and had managed to achieve a non-alignment status, and was entering the tourism stakes. British European Airways decided to back this enterprise and started a scheduled air service to Belgrade. The inaugural flight in a Viscount aircraft was planned for 2 June 1957, and a group of guests was assembled by Bill Simpson, headed by Earl Attlee, the former Labour Prime Minister of Britain, recently ennobled.

We duly flew to Belgrade with a call at Zurich on the way, and after a couple of days of formalities and entertainment in the capital, in which Laurence Olivier and his wife played a part, we set off in a rickety second-hand Soviet L12 (similar to a DC3) for Sarajevo. It was a unanimous decision of all of us, a dozen in number, to return to Belgrade by the night train two days later.

The Yugoslav Railways, locally faced with an apparent VIP party, found an elderly but plush and comfortable extra sleeper from some Sarajevo shed and attached it to the rear of the night train to the capital. We all had single berths, very pre-war and musty yet pleasantly cosy and suggestive of Edwardian travel in the *Orient Express*. The *Kriegslok*, sturdy and eight-coupled, had no trouble with the extra load and set off on the 310 mile journey at a steady 35-40mph, the maximum the recently repaired tracks of the time could allow.

I was aroused from a deep sleep, which had no doubt been prompted by heavy 'Slivovic'consumption the night before, in the small hours probably near Vinkovci. There were shouts and, indeed, screams coming from the corridor. In my pyjamas I opened my door, to find Bill Simpson in his pyjamas, and Lord Attlee, similarly clad, plus two ladies from our party. But Lord Attlee had lowered his trouser legs and Bill was staring at bare flesh. As I joined the group, the former Prime Minister shouted at me, 'You, too, Jones, look at my bottom.' Not having had such a request from a noble personnage before, I did so with some hesitation, to see the great man's rear covered with red lumps. One of the ladies shuddered and screamed again, whereupon the most ghastly screams came from another sleeping compartment.

Mrs Elizabeth Nicholas, for many years the travel editor of *The Sunday Times*, a large lady, emerged with her night dress in disarray. She was slapping at her buttocks, shouting. 'It's lice, it's bed bugs.' And it was.

The two victims, apparently only two out of twelve, eventually returned to their compartments but not to sleep. The rest of us searched our bunks, dozed a bit, but were glad to alight at Beograd at 6.30am!

# 50

# Guards on the Run

IT is by no means unusual for the train guards to be left behind at stations tops. This is more likely on suburban electric services with only one man in the cab and short station stops. In the days of steam it was the fireman's job to check back and confirm that all the train, including the guard, was safely proceeding out of the station. Nevertheless, it did happen even then.

I have mentioned in an earlier part of this book the tragic incident when a guard, who had been missing over a considerable length of the Great Northern main line, was found churned up in the wheels of the Gresley Pacific. This could only be explained later by a surmise that the guard had gone to the head of the train to check something and a member of the platform staff, fifteen coaches back form the locomotive, had improperly waved a green flag in addition to blowing a whistle.

In very recent times I have heard over the Victoria station announcements that 'the Tattenham Corner service is delayed awaiting a guard. We apologise for this, but the guard due to take the train was left behind at Streatham Common by the previous service and is on his way to Victoria by taxi'.

Frank Ferneyhough, that prolific recorder of railways in his many books, tells the story of a guard who always left his leap aboard the train until the last minute, priding himself on some macho ability. He worked a semi-fast Cambridge to Bletchley train, turning over his duty to another guard who took over for the run to Oxford.

He would run alongside his departing train and make a spectacular leap into the open door of his compartment at the rear. One morning at Woburn Sands station he collided with a passenger waving farewell to a friend. Both collapsed on the platform and the train, its front end enveloped in steam, moved rapidly in the direction of Bow Brickhill, the next station. There it was discovered that the guard was missing, but the engine crew decided to carry on to Bletchley where the relief man was waiting. The limping guard left behind at Woburn Sands was put aboard a short goods train which came through later and a telephoned explanation was made.

In due course, the guard received a reprimand by the district controller and was told in future to board his train before it actually started. Strangely, the fireman was brought before the local shedmaster and reprimanded for not checking his train.

On that same line linking the two great universities, now closed except for the Bedford-Bletchley stretch and freight-only line to Verney Junction and South to Aylesbury, Frank Ferneyhough tells of a prank which left a guard without boots.

During a particularly severe foot-and-mouth disease epidemic, a young man, neatly dressed and with an official-looking armband, boarded a train at Cambridge. Clutching a clipboard, he went along to the guards van and said, 'Sorry to bother you but regulations require that your boots be dipped in a disinfectant solution'. The luckless guard removed his boots and they were taken away with the comment that they would be brought back soon. The young man did return, carrying several pairs of shoes taken from embarrassed passengers. 'Look after these, guard, please.'

Suspicions developed when irate passengers found no

trace of a dip. The young man was under attack and threw some footwear out of the window before he was caught, along with a fellow prankster working further up the train. At Bedford they were taken before the station-master and action followed, which later included trouble at their Cambridge College, with some reparations to make. Unfortunately, the guard's boots had been among those thrown out of the window, and that luckless man had to do his job in socks until, eventually, another pair of boots was found which fitted him.

# 51

# A Regal Glance
# at King's Cross

I T was the Wednesday before Easter, 1969. In those days
car-sleeper trains left from King's Cross for Edinburgh,
together with a battery of sleeper trains to other parts of
Scotland and even to Newcastle-on-Tyne.

I had driven to the London terminus to arrive shortly
before ten o'clock at night, and met my old friend Frank
Ferneyhough, the railway writer, rail historian, and
public relations manager for special services. The car was
duly handed over at the loading bay with its keys in the
possession of a railwayman.

We walked back to the departure platforms of King's
Cross, and saw that the Royal Train was drawn up to the
buffers with a red carpet laid on the platform. It seemed
the Queen was going to Selby to present Maunday
Money the following day at Selby Abbey. Although
secure there was not the degree of security experienced
these days, twenty-three not very happy years on, and
my train was standing in the platform parallel to that of
the Queen's regal ukase.

After chatting to Frank for a while I entered my sleeper
and changed into pyjamas. The train was due to leave in
a few minutes. I pulled up my blind and knelt up on the
bed to look across at the Royal Train and to observe our

departure. The sleepers were, of course, the older, wider and more comfortable type known to generations of travellers, but they lacked the sound-proofing and air conditioning found today.

As I looked abeam I suffered an embarrassing shock which even today can bring out the makings of a cold sweat when I think about it. Her Majesty had entered her own quarters directly across from me and the blinds were not drawn. She looked through the window and saw me. whereupon she started to smile. What one should do in such circumstances I do not know - it was fourteen years before the intruding Irishman sat on her bed at Buckingham Palace - but in some panic I got down on the floor and dragged down the blind.

# 52

# Funerals on
# the Narrow Gauge

IT was a grey, cool day on 1 April 1981 when a group of us led by London Midland Region officials assembled at Aberystwyth station for the first public run of the season on the Vale of Rheidol line.

At that time, operation of this fractionally under 2ft gauge system was controlled from Stoke-on-Trent. The management had decided on a face lift, with the three tank engines repainted, one in blue and two in Brunswick Green. These three engines were the very last steam locomotives owned and operated by British Railways at that time although now the Vale of Rheidol has been sold to the Brecon and Methyr.

According to Beeching's successor in the Chair at the BR Board they must have been losing some £60 millions a year, since he stated publicly at a dinner at London's Savoy Hotel that, 'as soon as we have eliminated steam from BR we shall have eliminated the annual deficit.' Ironically, although BR does not actually own any steam engines today, the Inter City steam division leases up to sixty big engines, and makes a profit on their runs with the *North Wales Coast Express*, the *West Highlander* and elsewhere.

Anyway, ten years ago the Vale of Rheidol was a

London Midland working, supported by volunteer members of the narrow gauge line. Our party departed from Aberystwyth in fine style, belting up the valley behind *Prince of Wales*. After some twenty minutes, we came to a stop on a precipice with a dramatic view over a wide ledge, and here we were asked to disembark and gather reverently in front of the simmering engine. From the first coach a few men in black clothes emerged bearing an urn. This they carried to a pre-prepared aperture in the rock and set it in place.

'That's the first funeral,' said our leader from Stoke-on-Trent. 'The first train up to Devil's Bridge carries the ashes of enthusiasts who have died during the winter and who have expressed a wish to be buried on the line they have supported for so long.'

We did indeed stop a second time, just outside Rheidol Falls Halt, and repeated the sad process. These ashes would overlook a favourite view of the enthusiast who had enjoyed it for so many years.

# 53

# Great Central Riches

CELEBRATING the 150 anniversary of the first tour taken by Thomas Cook in 1841 from Leicester to Loughborough, a massive gathering of people assembled on the restored Great Central station at Loughborough. It was a hot July day in 1991, and the actor playing the part of Thomas Cook sweltered in the open as he made his speech,watched by people who tried to get in the shade of the station roof.

Then it was the turn of the railway, to haul many hundreds of people to Rothley where a gigantic lineside barbeque was being held. Beautifully restored Merchant Navy Pacific *Canadian Pacific* hauled the long train on its five mile journey.

Neither speeches nor conversation was possible during the meal due to tremendous sounds from the steam operated fairground organ. This was why we who were engaged in eating did not hear the *Rocket* Replica arrive with a couple of open passenger trucks. The ancient train stood alongside *Canadian Pacific*.

Coinciding with the 'Cook 150' was to be the opening of the extended Great Central Railway to a new terminus at Leicester North, near where Belgrave and Birstall station used to be, some two and a half miles north of the centre of Leicester. All the Cook guests, plus a great many more people invited by the Great Central Railway, embarked at Rothley for the journey over the extension. VIPs, in their stovepipe hats, and Mayors in their chains of office, climbed into the open trucks behind *Rocket*. Several hundreds enjoyed the comfort of *Canadian Pacific's* train of Mark 1 coaches. This followed *Rocket* to the bifurcation where double track into the new station permitted both trains simultaneously to break a tape.

But when we alighted and made our way to the rostrum, the sight of the *Rocket* passengers was an amazing one. Standing in their trucks they had received - on this hot, still day - the full benefit of the engine's exhaust. Their faces were black and their clothes smothered in smut. Both Mayors had to wipe their chains of office to show the gold!

A somewhat similar celebration occurred a century ago when Cooks were commemorating fifty years of service to the travelling public. That was in 1891, and incredibly at the banquet that followed the short trip to Leicester, Alderman Kempson, Mayor of Leicester, eighty-six years old, stood up to announce that he had been one of the passengers on the famous temperance excursion of 1841.

Gathered around the speakers at Leicester North station, which eventually is due to be built up to look a bit like Marylebone, we knew that a big donation was about to be made. Mr Peter Soulsby, leader of Leicester City Council, handed over a cheque to the Great Central Railway for £100,000. This was for the preserved railway's effort in spearheading a drive for tourism.

Then came two unexpected (at least for us, the spectators) donations. One came from Mr David Clarke, a local businessman, who had at one time worked as a signalman on the Great Central section of British Railways. He handed over £75,000.

Mr Michael Heseltine, Secretary of State for the Environment, leapt to his feet with a 'Tarzan' gesture. He and his City Action Team could not be in second place, was his announcement. For creating up to forty-five new jobs and giving the local people a sense of achievements - and restoring such a 'proud beast' as the Merchant Navy Pacific gently simmering beside him Mr Heseltine handed over a cheque for £110,000 to the Earl of Lanesborough of Main Line Steam Trust.

So the Great Central Railway was richer by £285,000 at the end of the day, plus a great deal of goodwill. Thomas Cook, later a subsidiary of Midland Bank, was poorer by some £10,000, including the bills which it accepted for cleaning the clothes of the dignitaries, and the barbeque lunch. But at least it did not have to spend on drinks - in keeping with the Founder's temperance beliefs, no alcohol was served, even to a large and thirsty press contingent.

# 54

# A Curious Exit on the Calne Branch

A typical Great Western Railway branch line, worked in its latter days by the ubiquitous 0-4-2 tanks, was the 5 ½ mile link from Chippenham to Calne. It survived four years into the Beeching era, escaping the holocaust until the beginning of 1965. The Great Western actually developed it by building a couple of primitive halts along the way, one at Stanley Bridge and - not until the late 1940s - another a mile short of Calne which was called Black Dog.

The push-pull service was good and even on Sundays offered seven trains each way. But Black Dog was passed through at a modest speed unless notice was given to the Guard for alighting, or a flag or lamp was waved from the short wooden platform.

One very dark night in the winter of 1952 a young NCO in the Royal Air Force Transport Command was on his way back from weekend leave to meet a Base pick-up at Calne. From Chippenham he had travelled in the same compartment, on this Sunday night, as an elderly lady dressed in black. Evidently she had told the guard that she wanted to alight at Black Dog, as the engine shut off steam and came to a stop at the halt.

The glimmer of a lamp hanging from the tiny shelter

showed the NCO that the platform serving the single track was on the left hand side of the train. But the elderly lady, gathering a small bag, made to get out on the other side. The Air Force man rose and tried to stop her but she waved him away with a grimace, opened the door, and stepped out into the night. But she did not fall; somehow she was on a platform, for the compartment lights showed her standing there, and she lifted a wrinkled hand as the train made a spirited start for its last mile of run.

The NCO puzzled over this mysterious exit for a month, and when the time came for another leave, which started in early March daylight on a Friday afternoon, he opened the train window and looked out carefully on the off-side as his Chippenham-bound train ambled slowly through Black Dog Halt. He saw a tiny structure not more than six feet across at the top, with steep steps leading down to the ground. Somehow the old lady had stepped on to it, but how could she have been sure it would be opposite her compartment?

Returning off leave on the Sunday night, the Air Force man saw the old lady, dressed again in black, on Chippenham station. They boarded the same two-coach push and pull, the 9.15pm for Calne, and he made sure of entering the compartment she chose.

Both were silent during the ten minute downhill run to Black Dog, where the train slowed and stopped. Again the old lady, to the NCO's alarm, got up and stepped out into the night. She was still standing on the tiny wooden structure as the engine accelerated away, leaving him more puzzled than ever.

Four weeks later, on his April 48 hours leave, he waited on Chippenham station for the branch line train to load, and again saw the old lady, dressed as she had been on the two previous occasions. He followed her into the same compartment saluting and saying 'good evening', to which she grunted.

He had to solve the mystery. He felt uneasy, almost as if he were in the presence of a Witch. Bolstering up his nerve, he asked her straight out, just after the train left Stanley Bridge Halt (a scheduled stop). 'Why do you get out on the wrong side at Black Dog? And how do you know you can step on to that small platform?'

She looked at him for a moment and then cackled: 'We live over on that side. Saves a bit of a walk. My son always sees to it we stop just right for this compartment. I always ride in this one. I'd tan his hide if he didn't put me down right. He's the driver, you see...'

# 55

# Selhurst Fantasies Come True

IN the very early 1930s, Selhurst station, on the Southern Railway main line from Victoria to Brighton and just a mile on the London side of East Croydon, was a choice spot for small rail enthusiasts. During a couple of hours on a Wednesday afternoon, a great variety of locomotives would come through at speed, shutting off steam as they reached the Gloster Junction curve towards East Croydon. Central Section 'Arthurs' with their six-wheel tenders, Brighton Atlantics, 'Remembrance' class Baltic tanks just before rebuilding, Moguls, 'Atlantic' tanks on the Oxted line trains, headed the busy traffic. Frequent suburban electrics used the two slow lines and rarely fouled the main.

It was in the autumn of 1931, as I dimly recall it, that my friend and I were talking about the long years of work on the Brighton Line by a class of engine we had never seen - the 0-4-2 'Gladstones'. We knew that the actual locomotive of that name had been retired after 45 years of service, and was now preserved, courtesy of the LNER, at York Railway Museum, a sturdy success aided by the Stephenson Locomotive Society. What about 'Fratton' and some of the others? Were they still steaming somewhere on the system?

The answer came like a fantasy come true as a train of non-corridor Brighton bogies passed under the Pawsons Road Bridge from Thornton Heath, headed by a 'Gladstone'! The 0-4-2 tender locomotive, in Southern green, thundered through Selhurst at about 50 miles an hour. We were flabbergasted, and not really quite sure what we had seen. We went over to the main platform and asked for our acquaintance, the station master. That worthy said we should not have been on the island platform spotting; with platform tickets we were safer on the wider main one. But he confirmed that we had seen a 'Gladstone' engine 'out on a final run - the Boss himself (Sir Herbert Walker) was aboard the train'.

We fantasised about it, as small boys will. I remember saying that the *Flying Scotsman* might yet come through. 'If it does,' I said, 'I'll be on the footplate.'

Some thirty four eventful years passed. Steam was fast fading and on the Brighton Section it was already a memory. But a Mr Alan Pegler of Retford had bought the famous Gresley Pacific *Flying Scotsman*. Under the terms of his contract, he was able to run her in many parts of the country. In 1965 he chose Brighton.

It was an autumn Saturday, nearing six o'clock in the evening, when we converged upon Brighton's superb terminus station to find No 4472 *Flying Scotsman*, resplendent and without her double tender, simmering at the head of a rake of British Railways standard coaches.

The right-away was given at a minute past six, and the train, packed with enthusiasts, started on its 60 minute run to Victoria. Alan Pegler was on the footplate of his engine. He had offered trips on the footplate over various sectors and I had been allocated South Croydon to Balham. Change-overs were, of course, possible due to the corridor tender.

Trailing her famous plume of smoke, *Flying Scotsman* made good time, sweeping across the famous Ouse Viaduct, where we glimpsed a large turn-out of spectators from Ardingly School. Thundering through Gatwick Airport station we reached 82 miles an hour at the Horley dip, the top speed of the run.

Starting on the dark and narrow passage through the tender shortly after the train passed Purley Oaks at speed, I arrived on the footplate on the approach to South Croydon, with the Oxted line coming in to the right of us. East Croydon was taken at a modest 40 miles an hour, hordes of platform watchers waving or staring in amazement. Accelerating round the curve, we charged through Selhurst at slightly better than fifty. That was the culmination, then, of a wild dream of 1931; I rode through Selhurst station on the footplate of *Flying Scotsman*.

# 56

# Sovereigns along the Dee

THE Great Western Railway proudly claimed to be the 'Royal Road' and there is little doubt, due to its line to the elaborate terminus at Windsor, that it carried more Crowned Heads than any other. But there was one system, very much smaller, which made a speciality of Royal trains. This was the Great Northern of Scotland, with its 43½ miles of Deeside line from Aberdeen to Ballater (the station for Balmoral Castle).

The GNSR was the only Scottish company to maintain Royal coaches. Normally, the Royal train would come to Aberdeen from the south and only need to be hauled to Ballater by Great North engines. But in Queen Victoria's reign there were many regional journeys to be made, such as one in 1872 all the way to Dunrobin to stay with the Duke of Sutherland, so locally provided Royal coaches were used. The company even sent its Royal coaches all the way to Doncaster – deep in England – to bring King Edward VII to Ballater.

Queen Victoria made at least four journeys a year on the Great North line, at first to Aboyne when the tracks ended there and later to Ballater. An extension planned to Braemar was never built, even though given the go-ahead as late as 1918. A concrete road was already under construction and motorised road transport was already raising its competitive head.

But it was not only the British Monarchy which used the Aberdeen to Ballater railway. The first foreign crowned head to be conveyed was the Shah of Persia in 1889. The King of the Belgians made two return journeys, while others who travelled included the King and Queen of Spain and the King of Portugal. But the most memorable was the journey of the Tsar and Tsarina of Russia, in September 1896. They arrived by the Russian Royal Yacht at Leith, to be met by the Great North's Royal coaches.

There were security problems even in those days, mainly from the Irish Fenians. The Great North arranged for men to be posted within sight of each other along the whole route. No pilot engine was run ahead of the Royal train (as happened in England) but on the single line stretches no train was allowed for at least 20 minutes before it was due to pass. On double track sections, all train meeting it had to slow to 10 miles an hour. All facing points had to be clipped and padlocked, and all level crossing gates locked until the Royal special had passed.

The weather was particularly bad for the whole of the trip by the Russian crowned heads, as bad as only the East Coast of Scotland can, on occasions, be with fierce northeasterly wind and constant driving rain. The decorations at various stations were ruined and mud sloshed everywhere. The unhappy lookout men were drenched and sometimes lost sight of each other.

In the Royal Saloon the Tsar is reported to have asked where the armed guards were. 'Armed guards, Your Imperial Majesty?' An aide was shocked. 'We do not need guns to protect you. The men along the line are good with their fists if they have to be.' The Tsar, unlike royalty in Britain and all over the rest of Europe in those days, insisted on being accompanied by an armed bodyguard. There was one, riding on the train, but he was Russian.

This same Tsar Nickolas was the Russian monarch who later visited King Edward VII at Sandringham, travelling by Royal train to Wolferton. On one occasion he went out on a long walk with King Edward who persuaded his guest to leave his armed bodyguard behind. 'I don't use a detective here at Sandringham Estate, and you don't need to either.' But history records that they lost their way and eventually came out of the woods onto a rough road. Here a carrier with his horse and cart was met with, and a lift back to Sandringham requested. The carrier said he was not going all the way but would take them to North Wootton station.

'We can take a train back to Wolferton from there, explained King Edward VII to his Russian guest. 'It is only three miles. I shall send for a carriage to meet us at Wolferton.' He then introduced himself and the Imperial guest to the carrier, with an exchange which has become a classic. 'I am the King of England and this is the Tsar of all the Russians.' 'Glad to meet you,' was the reported reply of the driver. 'I am the Archbishop of Canterbury.'

# 57

---

# Choke-up to D-Day

---

JOURNEYS from the West Midlands, Wiltshire, Somerset and Gloucester to Southampton and Portsmouth were difficult indeed in the weeks before 6 June 1944. They remained hard and slow until re-inforcements had been transferred to the South Coast and over to France.

The author experienced one of the slowest rail journeys he had ever known following a two day trip to Bath, undertaken from Portsmouth on a brief leave for urgent domestic reasons. 'Is your journey necessary?' asked the posters at that time. Well, mine was. And I got there on time with a through train from Portsmouth to Bath via Salisbury, running against the flow. But coming back, diverted via Limpley Stoke, held at places like Westbury and Salisbury, sent on to Romsey and Eastleigh, the foodless ride lasted from 4.30pm on the Sunday to 5.30am on the Monday.

It seems that was nothing compared to what happened on the Didcot, Newbury and Southampton line. This route became seriously overworked during the immediate build-up to D-Day. Although the loop lines had been hastily lengthened, the single track section between Newbury and Winchester (where the Great Western Railway had its own station at Cheesehill), a distance of 26¼ miles, remained a desperate bottleneck. Just as bad was the short section on from Cheesehill to the junction with the Southern Railway.

Apparently, on the occasion so many trains were squeezed into a primitive loop and siding that the signalman panicked and believed he had a form of grid-lock, nothing at all being able to move until something else had first moved out of the way. At times the line was kept open continuously which meant twelve-hour turns for the signalmen, and when it came to change turns at the weekend it sometimes happened that only a few hours relief was provided between two long turns. This on a line which, a year before, had only five trains each way daily for passengers and two pick-up goods. The Monday before D-Day had the heaviest traffic, with military and other specials following one another, and the normal train service also trying to operate.

Nodding off on duty in the boxes was not an unheard-of, though any signalman could be brought back from his reverie by the sound of a single call-attention bell on the block instrument. Not unnaturally, sleepy signalmen would occasionally be forgetful. A much frowned-on offence was failing to send two bells – train entering section. But there was an even more serious one of handing the single line token taken off an up train to the driver of a down one without passing it through the block instrument and obtaining permission.

Rumour had it that at a station (whose name was only very quietly whispered) an up freight had been given the block but 'train entering section' had not been received when early on a misty Monday morning the signalman eating his breakfast heard the sound of an approaching locomotive. 'Damn it, he's not given me two bells,' muttered the signalman to himself. He prepared to do a verbal battle with his mate at the next box down the line. So he pulled off the home signal, finished his dried egg (scrambled) and was then surprised to find no goods train wiggling its way into the loop. At that very moment two bells rang to say that the freight was even now only just entering the section.

At first the signalman thought he must be dreaming but then there came a blast on a whistle, from the other end of the loop. Had a ghost walked up the stairs of the box at that moment, he would not have been more surprised – or scared. He of course looked towards the other end of the loop, and there clearly showing through the mist was a 2–6–0 Great Western Mogul snorting away, its driver wondering why he was being kept waiting.

That driver was, in fact, kept waiting quite a bit longer, while the signalman telephoned angrily to the man in charge of the next box up the line. 'What do you mean by sending a train down without even asking me?'

The other signalman sounded repentant at first 'Oh hell don't tell anyone, will you I remember now. I forgot. I had the token already and assumed I'd put it through.' Then his mood changed. 'Well, who are you to complain? If I didn't give you "train-out-of-section" for the passenger, how is it you haven't asked what's happened to it? Are you happy for it to disappear into thin air?'

All the traffic got through, nearly half a million men were shifted mostly down the line without casualties (even though one in six became a casualty or a prisoner a few days later), and the single track route contributed significantly to the success of the Normandy landings. Today it is hard to find any trace of it, closed as it was just pre-Beeching in 1960, and few recall its pleasant stations (Woodhay, Highclere, Burghclere, Litchfield, Whitchurch, Sutton Scotney, King's Worthy, and the Cheesehill station in Winchester).